Song of Songs

The Journey of the Bride

Brian Simmons

insight *i* publishing group

Tulsa, Oklahoma

What Others are Saying About
Song of Songs—The Journey of the Bride

"An apostolic stone for the foundation is how I would describe this excellent manuscript, *Song of Songs*, by Brian Simmons. These truths are foundation stones for the end-time purpose of God since they address important issues such as: revival, spiritual gifts and ministries, apostles and prophets, house churches, power evangelism, intercessory prayer, etc. However if all these stones were in place, the foundation would still be incomplete. The greatest relational force in existence is God's love expressed through His Son to mankind. The response of the Bride of Christ to that love is the missing stone that must be in place before the Bridegroom returns. This is what *Song of Songs* is all about, and the truth of its pages is an apostolic word of exhortation to the church. The message of the book is a godly call to the Bride of Christ to make herself ready by discovering the extravagant love of Jesus, and abandoning herself to that love; as Brian says, 'take a journey into the heart of Jesus.' A key truth of the book is that the love of Jesus for His Bride is perfect regardless of our personal state of maturity. Maturity will come as we run after Him; we are called to go from knowing about Him to knowing Him—and loving HIM with all our heart. *Song of Songs – The Journey of the Bride* is a book of end-time truth, and I recommend it to every believer."

Dale Rumble
Author and church planter

"Thank you for the *Journey of the Bride...* It is the best book I have ever read on the Song of Songs! I believe it is a book for our times and is much needed in the Body of Christ today. This book is a "keeper" and will become a valued classic. There is an anointing that brings the reader into the presence of the Lord. It is sprinkled with salt—for it creates a thirst for more of the Living Water of His Holy Spirit."

Shelvey Wyatt
Transformation Ministries

"This book has within it the gold nuggets of the spiritual life. Brian's gift is to lovingly express them with a simplicity that pierces through to the riches many through the centuries have experienced on their love journey. His gentle words invite the heart to run toward, to reach, to move in and come into the dwelling place of the heavenly bridegroom's heart. There one burns to know him intimately. While meditating and communing throughout this commentary, the heart is enflamed with a greater passion for Jesus. It is drawn to give all to have him and give all for him, who is our pearl of great price. With pure love His longings for us fill our whole being and we cry to Him, "Draw me, my beloved!"

Carlotta Maria
AGAPE House

SONG OF SONGS: THE JOURNEY OF THE BRIDE

Song of Songs: The Journey of the Bride by Brian Simmons
Published by Insight Publishing Group
8801 S. Yale, Suite 410
Tulsa, OK 74137
918-493-1718

Unless otherwise noted all scripture quotations are taken from the New International Version of the Bible. Copyright © 1973, 1978, 1984 by International Bible Society. Used by permission of Zondervan Publishing House. Scripture quotations marked NAS are taken from the New American Standard Bible. Copyright © 1960, 1962, 1963, 1968, 1971, 1972, 1973, 1975, 1977, 1995 by the Lockman Foundation. Used by permission.

ISBN 1-930027-65-6
Library of Congress catalog card number: 2002111055

Printed in the United States of America

Dedication

To my beloved Congregation of
Gateway Christian Fellowship
A radical people who love the fire of God
You who have refreshed my heart
And become a joy to my spirit...
To you this book is affectionately
Dedicated.

"His banner over me is love."

Table of Contents

Preface

Come with us on a journey . . . *a mystical journey into the heart of Jesus.* Mysterious . . . incomprehensible in its fullness—this is the Song of Songs! You are about to be touched by the greatest prophetic song ever sung. The human author, King Solomon, wrote 1,005 songs, but nothing as heavenly and anointed as this (I Kings 4:32). Inspired by the Holy Spirit, this book is designed to disciple us into the image of Christ. We will see Jesus as the Refiner and His love as the flame—making us into pure gold.

We discover in this Song the power of prophetic words spoken into our destiny. All eight chapters overflow with prophetic affirmation that Jesus sings over His Bride. The story is of King Solomon who encountered a maiden from Shunem watching her flock. They fall in love and she became his bride. It is a story of a "nobody" who captured the heart of the King and is groomed to become his Princess Bride. It is an allegory, a story using symbolic language to present deeply spiritual truths . . . a vivid story about our journey into the heart of Jesus. Love meets us at each step. We are tested, yet affirmed. Trials surround us, but so does His strong arm. The Shulamite fails, and so do we. Nevertheless, the love of this marvelous Bridegroom-King never ends.

You are the one loved by the King in this story. Be careful not to miss that. It is easy to read this Book and apply it to someone else. Read the Song of Songs as though it were a duet sung by you and the Lord Jesus right there in your living room! These words of love will free your heart to live for Him. See in this story an example of how our soul grows in bridal affection for the Son of God until we are consumed in the fires of His holy love.

A few bold ones have ventured forth to write on the Song of Songs in recent years. Mike Bickle has compiled an excellent set of teaching notes that are groundbreaking in their scope. We are grateful for this "forerunner" who has gazed into the sacred mysteries, sharing with us what he has learned. And there are others. Robert Weiner, Watchman Nee, Madame Guyon, and Hudson Taylor; they have all blessed the Church with their gleanings. We must also mention the penetrating thoughts of one admired by many, a voice for the martyrs, Richard Wurmbrand. Every student of the Song of Songs should pick up a copy of his stirring book, *The Sweetest Song*. To receive the clearest understanding of the *Journey of the Bride* we recommend you follow the text in your Bible and refer often to the inspired Word as you "pray-read" through the story. Use the Song of Songs in your daily devotional life.

I believe that the love relationship revealed in the writing of Solomon *will* be granted to the end-time Bride of Christ. The Holy Spirit has given us glimpses into the higher realms of the Spirit that we have never touched — only to draw us on until we cannot live without more. This is the strategy of God to make us lovesick friends of Jesus. Our spirits groan to be clothed with the robes of His favor and revelation. Let us lay aside unbelief and take this book as our very own road map into the flaming heart of Jesus!

Brian Simmons

Introduction
How to Interpret Song of Songs

Within the Song of Songs lies the heartbeat of Jesus Christ . . . and His yearning to bring forth a Bridal Partner to share His throne. If you listen carefully, you will hear His heartbeat in every chapter. Jesus wants you to be His friend, one that can enter into a mature relationship with Him. He wants to share His life, His power, and His glory with those who are determined to be His friends. Jesus shares secrets with His friends . . . but He must be convinced of our willingness to seek Him.

The Shulammite maiden represents this kind of seeking love. She hears a *prophetic* song that reveals God's fiery heart of love. You cannot read this book without being captured by the majestic personality of our King. The testimony of Jesus comes forth in this Song. It takes up where all other songs have ended. We hear the heart of the Bridegroom singing His thoughts and feelings about us . . . His Bride to be.

The author of the Song is a mystic . . . and he freely uses the language of mysticism to describe the love of the Heavenly Bridegroom for His Bride. Some rivers flow quietly between their banks, others overflow. This is a river overflowing, a cup running over, a heart in which the love of God burns. These notes are written for hearts like that — hearts that long and cry out for the deep.

We encourage you to read the Song of Songs devotionally, praying over the Scriptures and making them your own. Look up the Scriptures we have given to help you understand the meaning of the text. Recently, while teaching this book to missionaries, the Holy Spirit spoke to me saying, *"I love this Book. I inspired it. It is my desire to exalt the Son of God with every word of this Book."* There is a fierce loyalty in the Holy Spirit to exalt the Son. God's Spirit longs to fill His people with love for Jesus. Cooperate with the Holy Spirit as you read through these notes. Let the spark of His fiery love burn within you.

In the **Zohar** (The Light), the main book of the Kabbalah, the work which contains the Jewish mystical traditions, it is written concerning this portion of Scripture:

> *The Song of Songs is superior to all songs that preceded it. . . . Other men send up praises by means of lower chariots, but King Solomon by means of higher chariots. . . . On the day when this song was revealed the Shekinah (God's Glory) descended to the earth, as it is written, 'And the priests could not stand to minister because of the cloud.' Why? Because the glory of the Lord had filled the Temple (I Kings 8:11). On that day this hymn was revealed, Solomon sang this song in the power of the Holy Spirit. . . . It is a song, in which those who are above and those who are below participate; a song formed in the likeness of the world above, which is a supernatural Sabbath, a Song through which the supernal Holy Name is crowned. Therefore it is the Holy of Holies. Why so? Because all its words are full of love and joy!*

In the **Babylonian Talmud** (another sacred book of the Jewish people), the following words were spoken by Rabbi Akiba: *"No day in the history of the world is so precious as the day on which the Song of Songs was given to Israel; for all the other Scriptures are holy, but the Song of Songs is the holiest of all."*

How to Interpret the Song of Songs

There are different schools of thought about interpreting the Song of Songs. God has creative abilities far beyond our understanding, He is able to speak on many different levels at the same time. Here are some of the more widely accepted interpretations of this book:

1. Natural Interpretation – The book displays a human love story between a man and his bride without any figurative spiritual meaning.

2. Jewish Historical Interpretation – The book shows the relationship between God as the Bridegroom and natural Israel as the Bride (Jer. 2:2, Hos. 2:16-20).

3. Allegorical Interpretation – The book tells a story that is totally symbolic without any historical facts as its basis. The natural details of the story are not factual but point to spiritual truths. We believe that to understand the Song of Songs you must realize the story line.

4. Typological Interpretation – The book shows the details of the story as a 'type' or picture that reveals deeper spiritual meaning with symbolism. The symbol is not nearly as important as the truth it represents.

For the most part, I have chosen the *Allegorical/Typological* method of interpreting this sacred writing. At times I have broken from traditional thought and given my own sense of what the Spirit of God is showing me. Clearly, this is a story about Jesus loving His Bride into maturity. In her weaknesses, in her insecurities, in her failings, she is loved. That assurance releases power for transformation. Perfect love will cast out fear—fear that keeps us trapped the way we are.

The Three Main Characters

1. King Solomon—depicted as a type of the triumphant, resurrected Lord Jesus *(King of Peace)* who reigns as King and reveals Himself to His friends as the Heavenly

Bridegroom. His supreme passion for the Bride shines forth from this inspired story.

2. The Shulammite Maiden — depicted as a type of the Bride of Christ, who is prepared to be a co-heir of all things, seated on the Throne with Him for all eternity. She begins as a Maiden and becomes the mature Bride. We believe it is the individual believer, awakened to Bridal passion, who is the Shulamite.

3. The Daughters of Jerusalem — seen as a type of those who love and honor Jesus, but have not yet attained the maturity of passion seen in the Bride. Many scholars conclude that they represent believers who love God, who have not yet grown up into the fullness of Christ (Eph. 4:13-16). The story does not begin with the initial salvation experience but with the awakening of passion for Jesus. As the story ends, these "daughters" are also awakened to holy passion and begin to "run after" Him, forming a sacred circle of the "Shulammite spirit" imparted to others.

Also included in the story line are the "angry brothers" who often misrepresent the maiden's lovesickness and cannot understand her extravagant devotion to the Bridegroom. And there are "watchmen" mentioned in the story and fall into two different categories:

- Those godly servants of the Body of Christ who point others to the Bridegroom.

- The watchmen who are found wounding the Bride and taking away her "cloak."

Solomon's Song of Songs

Song of Songs 1:1
ॐॐ

The Divine Kiss

Chapter 1:1-4
ಬಿCG

Jesus loves to sing over you . . .

*D*id you know you bring Him so much joy He has to sing about it? Can you imagine Jesus Christ singing over you with passion and celebration? What would He sing? What are the lyrics of His Song? If you listen . . . really listen . . . you can almost hear the melody. . . .

"He will rejoice over you with singing" (Zeph. 3:17).

Today, open your heart as the Holy Spirit calls you to take a bold step into the **Journey of the Bride**. Your journey will lead you into the same pathway as the Shulamite. Her journey will be your journey. Along the way you will be blessed and broken, filled and knowing failure, cherished and challenged. And in the end . . . you will be consumed with Him!

The Song of Songs is a divine opera, the most powerful piece of music ever written. It is a Song written by King Solomon almost three thousand years ago . . . a Song that tells an incredible story. Incredible, because it is yours! It has been included in our Bible to lead you into the flaming heart of Jesus Christ. Once you have heard the music, nothing else can make you dance. . . .

Our story begins with a cry from a passionate heart: **"Let Him kiss me with the kisses of His mouth."** This is what every heart cries out for . . . the *Divine Kiss*; sacred intimacy with Jesus Christ. Kisses from God impart the deepest things that could ever be given to the human spirit. This "kiss" is the answer of why we are on the earth. The Lord kissed Adam and he became a living soul . . . and so we come alive again by this **kiss of God.**

Your Creator knows that true transformation comes in a relationship where love's torrent covers our sin and makes us lovely in His sight. Just as relationships in the past had the power to wound and scar our souls, downloading lies into our thinking . . . so a passionate pursuit of the Bridegroom holds the key for the deepest level of change in our personalities.

Jesus does not come to scare us into submission, but to woo us into friendship with Him. God delivered His transforming truth and the grace for change in a *relational* package; the person of His Son. Grace has a face; and His face is smiling.

It seems so unrealistic that the uncreated God loves us so deeply and is ravished by our gaze! The God of heaven actually seeks voluntary lovers, not trembling slaves. Jesus wants your hand in marriage . . . male or female; for we are all a part of the Bride of Christ. Walls that keep us from intimacy must come down. We often hide behind a wall of our ugly feelings about ourselves. . . .

Jesus sees in you a suitable companion that will flood His heart with joy for all eternity. Fill your mind with the truth of how God sees you. Others will always judge you by your greatest weakness. God sees the glory of His Son shining in you.

Our own hearts tell us we are not worthy; "I am a bad person in so many ways." How true . . . but irrelevant. The love of your King has stepped out of eternity.

His love is totally unrelated to how you have behaved the past week. Since His love is an eternal love, it will not end the first time you fail. Even immature believers are a great delight to Him! His steadfast love will keep you near Him no matter what. His love endures forever (Ps. 118:1); enjoy all of it you can!

Try praying this way . . .

> *"Lord, its me – your favorite one!*
> *I am the one You love."*

You must identify yourself as a disciple whom Jesus loves, just like the apostle John did (John 13:23). John claimed for himself that identity, and so must you.

Listen to Jesus when he says:

Just let me love you. Don't try to re-negotiate your relationship with Me every time you fail. Come before Me just as you are. Call yourself My favorite, the one I love! I have made none other like I have made you. I love you endlessly, passionately – in your best moments and in your not-so-best moments. You really are my personality type. I have made you to be My friend.

We must discover the glorious, completing love of God. If you are single, you do not have to find a mate to discover love. If you are in a difficult, unfulfilled marriage, you do not have to go outside the boundaries to discover love. If you are a known sinner who has struggled with disgraceful habits and thoughts – there is a love waiting for you that will sweep you off your feet. It comes to us like a kiss from heaven. There are places in your heart that will only be healed by Divine romance . . . so run into Abba's arms today and abandon yourself to Him!

If you could ask for anything in prayer today, *this* is what to ask for: **"Let Him kiss me!"** She does not ask for a sermon, or for success, for a reward or for information, not even for a miracle . . . she simply wants to be kissed by the Divine.

Does He really want to be that close to me? Doesn't Jesus know what I'm really like? Your enemy, the accuser, will tell you that God will love you someday when you are perfect in heaven. But the Holy Spirit is saying to you today, "I love you even in your brokenness and weakness. You are my loving child. I was the One who kissed Adam and made him into a living soul. My kiss upon your heart will give you the love you seek. I will not abandon you the next time you fail. I am yours for all time and for all eternity."

Did you know that Jesus calls you one of His *glorious* ones? *"As for the saints who are in the land, they are my glorious ones in whom is all my delight"* *(Ps. 16:3).* As one of His "glorious ones" He does not wait until you are perfect before He enjoys you. He calls you a hero before you ever act nobly.

Today, Jesus smiles at the thought of you. He is the Lover of your soul. You really are His personality type, for He made you in His image!

"With the Kisses of His Mouth"

Don't think of Jesus actually kissing you on the mouth; rather, think of God awakening your heart with His power and love. Think of God's Spirit falling on you with a fresh passion to know your Bridegroom-King. This Spirit-kiss comes to us each time we open our hearts to the Word of God. A kiss is one of the most tender expressions of love known to man. Every person in the world can understand its meaning.

A *kiss* is the first thing we give to our newborn and the last thing we do with a loved one leaving this life. The longing for a kiss is deep in the heart of every human being. . . . We all want the tender show of affection from others. . . . but would Jesus love me that much? The words of His mouth are the superior pleasures of life. His heavenly kiss is not the joining of mouth to mouth, but the joining of God with man.

With His friend, Moses, God spoke *"face to face"* (Num. 12:8). But in the Hebrew language it says, "mouth to mouth." God spoke to Moses "mouth to mouth!" This is the Kiss of His Word to our spirits. It is the longing of the soul to be united to the Word of God.

We may say to our Friend, "Let the holy kisses of Your Word touch my heart today! Lord, breathe the Words of Your mouth into my heart. You have convinced me that you love me . . . convince me again!" The very measure of love Jesus has for you is the very measure of love the Father has for Jesus (John 15:9, 17:23). We are completing the circle of love that sits enthroned. . . .

We cry out to Abba and say, "Let Your Son, the Son of Your Splendor, let *Him* kiss me with the diverse **kisses** of His Word. Kisses of affection, kisses of mercy, kisses of forgiveness and reconciliation. I do not deserve to kiss your hand . . . not even your feet; yet you give me the kisses of your mouth . . . the kisses of your Word." Jesus responds with: *"I love those who love Me (Prov. 8:17)."*

Let *HIM* kiss me . . . not just His prophets. It must be the visitation of His words flowing from His mouth into mine (Ps. 119:131). Not a messenger or an angel, but Him. Not interpretations from His teachers, but the Word from His mouth.

Let *HIM* kiss me . . . the One beloved of His Father, kissed by His Father. When the Father kisses the Son it imparts the depths of infinite love, transcending anything known on earth. When the Son kisses you, His complete love fills you with a knowledge and depth of revelation that cannot be fathomed. When the Son of God kisses you with the Word of God you are changed forever (Gal. 1:11-12).

Nothing More Delightful

The maiden's cry for kisses brought Him near. She prayed to the Father that He would come with kisses; now she speaks directly to Him . . . **"Your love is more delightful than wine . . . "** The love of Jesus is the most pleasurable thing to the heart. Nothing is more delightful. Nothing can compare to His love.

Wine is a symbol of the pleasures of this world (Ps. 104:15). These pleasures are the *good things* God has provided for us. His better-than-wine-love is more pleasurable than every blessing known on earth. The "wine" of this world cannot touch me like His love. The joys of this world are from a muddy, dirty pool.

If only people knew there was a sweeter, cooler fountain to drink from . . . far more refreshing . . . the intoxicating love of Christ. Haven't you found His love delightful?

It is the wonder of wonders that the Son of God should love us. He was in glory with His Father for billions of years, needing nothing. He looked down on the earth and found us lost and lonely. . . . He left everything to make us His own. Can you drink in the sweetness of that thought? Unmerited love! He has loved you freely, without requiring anything in you to attract such love. He sought you, He bought you, and He brought you back.

Do you remember that day? **O, happy day!** Say to your Friend, **"Your love is more delightful than wine. . . . "**

The Shulamite maiden is seeing the absolute truth of this in her life. All is empty apart from Him. Eternal love has gripped her heart. You can drink too much wine, but you cannot have too much of His love (Eph. 5:18)!

She will no longer be led astray by the pleasures of an empty world. The divine kiss has caused her to forget all that is in the world. Fullness has overwhelmed her. She must know this love that is better than wine. His kiss reveals the holy words hidden in His heart... this is His wine . . . He pours it out for her.

The Hebrew text reads, "Your *loves*". . . . Christ's love for us is in the plural. There are many forms of His embrace that renew the human spirit. He offers us infinite, boundless love that has been with us before the world was formed.

Forgiving love, accepting love, providing love, guiding love, keeping love—"Your loves" are better than wine! A lovesick people will do anything for this love. There is no sacrifice; there is no pleasure this world has to offer that could compare to the affection of Jesus for YOU.

His Pleasing Perfume

The revelation of the personality of Jesus Christ is like the most pleasing perfume. The cologne of His compassion! What can compare to it? Can you smell His fragrance, sweeter than the rose? His perfume is His presence . . . it speaks of who He is, not of something He has done. His perfume speaks of what He thinks, what He feels. His personality, His internal qualities of love and gentleness have captured her. She is swept off her feet . . . lost in the perfumes of God! She understands the emotions of His heart.

Jesus' lovely personality is filled with passion and pleasure for His people. How pleasing to the troubled and tested ones in this life to know the sweet fragrance of the personality of Jesus Christ. **"Pleasing is the fragrance of Your perfumes. . . ."**

To smell His cologne, you must be close to Him. She has drawn near and is touched by His sweetness. She can tell by His countenance, by the look in His eyes, how much He enjoys her. She has never seen such love expressed before. He beams with love for her. His thoughts of her are real and kind. His invisible sweetness has touched her (Luke 7:47).

Wine and perfume . . . Jesus is the most pleasing beverage and the most intoxicating fragrance. She has tasted Him, and she has been lifted by even His scent. His anointing oils have touched her as she longs for more of His loveliness poured deep within.

She is motivated by this fragrance to rise and run with Him. The loving ways of Jesus are like the most pleasing perfume. We must repent of holding thoughts in our heart that are not true about God. The key that unlocks the heart is to understand the stunning personality of Jesus!

Pleasing is His personality . . . can you smell His cologne? Can you feel the pleasure of His kiss? Can you taste His wine?

The Sweetness of His Name

Just saying His Name is like opening the finest flask of costly perfume. *Jesus*. His Name touches us deeply. His character is revealed in that Name. His Name speaks of His works, His deeds, His character, His leadership. Just to think of Him opens our hearts to the sweetness of true love. His deeds are lovely and wise, appearing as fragrant oils. She is now realizing how wise and good He is with those who love Him. She cannot be offended with One who is perfect in all His ways. He knows what is best, He does what is best, and He always works in wisdom! More desirable than any other. . . .

"Your Name is like perfume poured out." God has poured forth the Name of His Son upon us. His is the only Name the Father has poured forth. When His Name is poured out like perfume, the lost become lovers of God. The anointing for ministry is found in the poured out Name of our Beloved. Let your Perfumed Name be poured out upon me, Lord Jesus!

The **"maidens"** are those believers who have yet to be gripped with holy passion for the Son of God. They are sincere and true believers but immature in their love. This entire story is the saga of how the maidens, following the king from a distance, become a "Shulamite" and begin their pursuit of the Bridegroom. The book will end where it begins. . . .

No wonder we adore Him . . . even the immature are cherished by Jesus. We must have more songs to sing about His love. The world must know that Jesus is a Friend to the sinful one. Lord, no wonder our hearts swell at the mention of Your Name! To see You is to love You. How worthy you are, Prince of Glory, to receive the love of all!

This Divine Song will awaken you to pursue your Divine Friend. Plead with Him to reveal more of His endless love, that you may give it all back to Him.

"How right they are to adore You!" An ancient translation reads, "Righteousness loves you." Jesus is everything that righteousness stands for. He is the perfect example of manhood, perfection, grace and uprightness. Those who are upright in heart will see in Him their perfect model and Spouse.

Her Life Vision

This is the prayer of awakened desire: **"Take me away with You . . ."** The maiden longs to be drawn away in sacred intimacy with the King. She verbalizes the longing in her heart to be changed; drawn out of her comfort zone, drawn away from sin and self. *"Draw me after You!"*

Nothing else can satisfy the thirst she feels. She is ready to make a break from everything else to follow Him. In spite of weakness, she longs to be drawn to Him . . . to be taken away from all that is unclean and impure. Is this your cry?

When we ask to be drawn after the Son of God we are asking that He be exalted to the highest place in our hearts. The maiden recognizes that spiritual growth is a response to God's drawing love as it tugs at her heart. None of us seek God apart from His tender influence on our spirits (John 6:44). His touch draws us to His heart, as He longs for us to know Him as He is.

Do you have a longing to be close to Jesus? Take this prayer into your heart and ask the Holy Spirit every day to draw your heart toward Jesus. Even if He has drawn you a thousand times in the past, ask Him to draw you again. Cultivate a friendship with Him. See yourself as His partner, His companion; one He wants to be with. He will be more to you than you can imagine.

"I will run after You."

Running with Jesus with all your heart is the only proper response when He draws you! It is an act of holy zeal. To run after Him will one day bring us into His arms. We will become holy partners, touching others with this love. Our heart cries, *"Draw me so that I may influence others. And while I am serving others, I will run after you."* We are drawn into intimacy so that we will be His partners in ministry. Passion for Jesus always results in compassion for others.

Jesus is on a mission . . . and He wants to include you. He is changing the hearts of people with the power of His love. The Son of God is longing for a Bridal

Partner, not just a girlfriend. He is looking for one who will run with Him to do the Father's business. Running represents obedience in action. We must hurry to do His will—not with a striving heart, but resting at His side.

Jesus will have a Bride at His side that will run with Him to touch the nations! This has become her life vision. Sadly, she later forgets this and refuses to run, choosing instead to remain in her comfort zone (2:8-13).

God wants us to join the passion of Mary with the servant heart of Martha. Mary and Martha were two sisters who once entertained Jesus in their home. While Martha was busy with "housekeeping" Mary chose the better part by sitting at Jesus feet. Martha had compassion for others but lacked the passion for Jesus that Mary had.

The Holy Spirit will help us to have both of these qualities in proper balance; intimacy with Jesus and compassionate service to others. As we sit at His feet long enough we will be willing to get our feet "dirty" in serving this world.

The apostle Paul is an example of one who had both the passionate heart of Mary and the compassion of Martha. Divine drawing and speedy running. . . . May we have it all! One day, if we will continue after Jesus with a running heart, our panting soul will find Him, and He will bring us into His secret place. . . .

The King's Chambers

The King's chambers? Jesus would take *me* into the dwelling place of a King? This Divine, celestial-chamber-room is where God carries us into special experiences of His grace. This is His secret, private chamber where He discloses Himself to the seeking heart. . . . It is the treasure-house of His heart. He does not bring us merely into the courtyard . . . but into His chambers; where we experi-

ence personal encounters with our King, and fresh impar-
tations of the Spirit in the secret place.

One day the patriarch Jacob saw a stairway leading
to these elevated chambers . . . He called it the House of
God, Bethel. These anointed experiences lead us into the
heart of Jesus . . . up the hidden stairway right into His
heart!

Only Jesus our King can bring us into the chamber
room where He dwells. **"Let the King bring me into His
chambers. . . . "** We enter not by our striving or maneu-
vering. He must bring us in by redeeming grace. Jesus is
the Shepherd who carries the lamb over His shoulders . . .
carried into His chambers (Luke 15:5). Still, we must pray
and ask Him to take us in and reveal His glory to us!

Divine fellowship in His sacred chambers awaits us.
There will be a banqueting table but for now we must be
alone with Him in His chamber room of intimacy. In this
place we receive the living Bread, the Manna of His presence that nourishes our spirits.

O, the sacred mysteries He reveals in His chambers!
Do you hear His invitation? Do you see the open door
(Rev. 4:1)? Can you trust Him to bring you in? Surely,
One so holy, One so beautiful as He would have better
friends than I. . . .

No longer reluctant or preoccupied, the maiden
wants to be where He is. "Take me into your palace of
glory, take me into your chambers, Lord Jesus—where I
can hear your message of love." In His chambers He will
share His secrets. Happy are those who are brought into
that wonderful place of revelation and impartation.

Imagine what this King could reveal to you if you
spent time in His chambers, where only trusted friends
were allowed to enter . . . exchanging friendship with a
King! The maiden cries out for kisses of intimacy and

promises to run with Him. He responds by leading her into the chamber room experiences of deeper revelation.

Every one of us must have a secret history in God, a hidden life in His chambers. This is where the Lord develops us and matures us in preparation for running with Him. Jesus has gone to prepare a place for YOU. That place is His chamber room full of power, revelation, and love. It is the hiding place prepared for you. . . .

The King's chambers are open to every seeking heart. In the King's chambers He will share His secrets with you. You will taste the delights of sacred intimacy. Don't think you must wait until heaven to be drawn into His chambers. Ask Him to bring you in today. Search for the chambers of the King (Ps. 45:13-15, Mark 14:14-15). You will find Him within the veil. . . .

The Daughters of Jerusalem Speak

The daughters of Jerusalem overhear this outburst of passion and they too are drawn into the delight of this King. They are stirred by the passion of a seeking heart, **"We rejoice and delight in You."** Every believer will one day be drawn into the spiritual realization of ecstasies that excel anything known on earth. It is called, "inexpressible and glorious joy (I Pet. 1:8)."

The one thing that will draw immature believers into pursuit of Jesus is a heart on fire. A "holy virus" is released when others see your undying love for the King. As you become His friend, others are excited about following Him in this way too. The daughters of Jerusalem are stirred to a new level of devotion as they see the maiden drawn to the King. Rejoicing in God is the result of new levels of passion for Jesus (Phil. 3:3).

"We will praise your love more than wine." So many things could come between our Beloved and us . . .

so many worldly sorrows and disappointments work to hinder us from rejoicing in His love. Our failures, our wandering hearts, our hard thoughts . . . yet "we *will* praise your love more than wine."

Away with sorrows! Away with disappointment! There is a love we can praise every day of our lives; the love of the King! As we drink the cup of communion, we remember the intoxicating sweetness of His love more than the wine. She resolves to make her "theology of love" more important than the pleasures of this life.

"How right they are to adore You." The Shulamite speaks this over her King as she is enthralled with His presence. It is right for all the world to adore Him. No wonder maidens (and brothers!) love Him. It is with good reason that every tender heart should adore him. The maidens are the hidden ones who are being prepared to be the Bride. . . .

The major theme of this book is the love of God and how His beauty can conquer and capture the human soul. His love conquers fear, unbelief, and the shame of failure. Rejection is drowned out by the strong current of love in His eyes. . . .

It is right for everyone to worship and adore the Son of God. Why do we want the kisses of His Word? Because we have tasted of His love. A deeper passion to know Him has gripped our hearts. *Are you ready for more?*

"Dark am I . . .
Yet Lovely!"

Song of Songs 1:5
಄಄಄

Her First Discovery

Chapter 1:5-8
ೞೞ

*P*assion for Jesus is the pathway into the heart of God. To fall in love with Jesus and to abandon our heart to Him is the noble threshold we must all cross on our journey into His heart. But to love Him will cost us everything. In the beginning, it seems like a fantasy . . . that He would come and enjoy such sacred intimacy with one like me.

Little do we know that loving Jesus will lead us not only into His heart, but also into trouble. To know Jesus is to be emptied of self, to be broken. The first crisis of our new life in Christ is to find out that we don't *have* problems, we *are* the problem . . . but wait till you hear what He tells us!

Brought into His chambers, the maiden discovers the darkness of her heart. The deeper we go into the heart of Jesus, the more we confront our own weaknesses and shameful ways. It seems as though we get worse rather than better. This is God's way of breaking us, showing us the weakness of our flesh.

In His chambers the maiden cries out, **"Dark am I."**[1] Her heart is corrupt and she knows it. This is the first crisis in her journey — the revelation of her own sinfulness. Each one of us must face this truth: we are fallen sinners of Adam's race. But as she bows her head in the presence of His splendor, she hears Him say, **"Yet lovely!"**

Could it be? Did He really call her lovely? Would Jesus call *me* lovely? But doesn't He know my heart . . . my weak heart? Yes, He knows all things . . . and still He calls *you* lovely.

Here's a secret: We are both *totally sinful* and *totally forgiven*. Place these two phrases together . . . **"Dark am I"**— **"Yet Lovely!"** The cry of the awakened heart is: **"I am dark and sinful!"** . . . But when we are brought into the King's chambers and stand in His presence we hear Him say . . . **"Yet Lovely."** The One who gazes into the human spirit knows that we love Him.

Every believer has two natures . . . two forces working inside. One can do no wrong, and the other can do no good! It is only when we accept this paradox of grace that we can be deeply healed by God's acceptance. If we focus only on our darkened soul we will soon grow depressed and introspective. If we focus on Christ and His view of our life, we will mature and give our life away to Him.

What makes us lovely to God? It could never be our performance. Our loveliness is found in the image of Jesus and a willing spirit that longs for Him. He loves us even when we are darkened by sin, with wrong desires and still with immature ways. He calls us lovely, because deep down we sincerely want to obey Jesus and know Him in fullness.

Abba's "anyway love" is here. He can say, "Yes, I know and you know that sin has brought shame, but *I love you anyway*. Your longings for Me make you lovely. With a willing spirit you will go on to mature bridal love."

God has infinite passion to see you through the growth process. He will not leave you halfdone! He is the God who finishes what He begins (Phil. 1:6).

Throughout life, every new "chamber room" experience will bring an even deeper understanding of unworthiness. You will cry out each time, "O, Lord; I am darkened by my sin." But if you listen carefully, you will also hear your King say, **"Yet lovely!"**[2] The voice she hears from the shadows whispers to her: "You may seem dark, but you are lovely to Me!" **Imagine the King bringing you into His chambers . . . Not to tell you what is wrong with you, but to tell you how lovely you are!**

The maiden sees herself **"dark like the tents of Kedar.**[3] "These tents were made from animal skins and were darkened by prolonged exposure to the sun. She again sees herself as a darkroom with no light shining in, full of the works of the flesh. However, listen to the King of Glory describe her: **"Like the tent curtains of Solomon."**

Solomon only used the finest of linen to make his tent curtains. He is saying to the Shulamite, "You see yourself dark and covered with shame, but let Me tell you what I think of you. You are as lovely as the white tent curtains that I use in my dwellings. You are like the finest linen curtains in the Holy of Holies!"

Only the priests could see the beauty of these curtains suspended in the Sanctuary of the Most High . . . only the living God knows your true worth, your true beauty. Outwardly they see only the dark tents, but inwardly your Bridegroom sees white linen.[4] Others may delight in seeing your distress and darkness. Your Lover-Friend delights in seeing your inner beauty.

Your own righteousness may be like the dark tents of Kedar, but the King of Glory sees far beyond our flesh to our spirits. He sees your glistening spirit like a gleaming white linen curtain hanging in the sanctuary of the Holy Place. This is truly who we are in Christ.

If we fail to hear that He calls us lovely, we will struggle with a cloud of uncertainty in our walk with Him. Our hearts must be filled with this awareness in order to pass the tests that will come. The confidence that Christ sees us as pure and lovely must fill us completely. Our Bridegroom-King embraces us in our weakness. We bring to Him our brokenness, He brings Divine forgetfulness. . . . What kind of King is this?

Why He Would Call Us Lovely:

The finished work of Jesus on the Cross. Our loveliness comes from the wonderful gift of righteousness that is ours when we believe (II Cor. 5:21). We are lovely in His sight because of what He did for us, not what we do for Him! You are ready for the King's presence. We have a King who gave away His beauty to take away our disfigurement. It is through the sacrifice of Christ that we are made lovely in His sight. The robe of righteousness that you wear has a designer label . . . "Made in Heaven Exclusively for the Bride of Christ."

The willing spirit that says "Yes" to God. The work of the Holy Spirit and our sincere intentions leaves us lovely in His sight! He will always define us, not by our weak flesh but by the willing spirit! He knows our love is immature, but He sees more than the outward failures; He sees the beauty of His life forming within you. A contrite and willing spirit moves the heart of God. You can fail in many areas, but a broken heart, He will not despise (Ps. 51:17).

The kindness of God's personality. The passions and pleasures that God feels toward us make us truly lovely in His eyes! He enjoys us even when we feel darkened by our failures. The loveliness of His personality washes us in His presence and clothes us in the clean garments of salvation.

The paradox of grace is this: We are in Adam, and we are in Christ.

The eternal destiny of becoming the Lamb's wife. We are the ones loved by God because He has chosen us to be the spouse of His Son. The first time Jesus laid eyes upon you He knew you would be His! What a mystery this is! Paul called it a "great mystery" concerning Christ becoming one with His Bride (Eph. 5:31-32). God is not your Father-in-law. . . . He is your eternal Father-in-LOVE! You are the love gift given to His Son (John 17:6).

The virtues of grace that only He sees. You possess in the most secret and hidden places of your life beautiful virtues that will one day be seen by all. For now, they are only *seeds* of the glory and life of your Lord. But in time, they will spring up in *radiant beauty.* His image is stamped within you and is reflecting back to Him . . . enriched with every grace and virtue, He sees beauty in your eyes! Listen to the voice of your Father as you read this:

> *I bathed you with water and washed the blood from you and put ointments on you. I clothed you with an embroidered dress and put leather sandals on you. I dressed you in fine linen and covered you with costly garments. I adorned you with jewelry: I put bracelets on your arms and a necklace around your neck, and I put a ring on your nose, earrings on your ears and a beautiful crown on your head. So you were adorned with gold and silver; your clothes were of fine linen and costly fabric and embroidered cloth. Your food was fine flour, honey and olive oil. You became very beautiful and rose to be a queen. And your fame spread among the nations on account of your beauty, because the splendor I had given you made your beauty perfect, declares the Sovereign LORD.*
>
> Ezekial 16:9-14

God's love is illogical. Paul states that it "surpasses knowledge" (Eph. 3:19). We can only know how God feels about us by revelation. The Holy Spirit must make it plain to our wounded soul: His love never fails. We are all fallen image-bearers. Destined for the throne, yet made from dust. Reaching for the sky, yet bowing down in shame. All of us must discover that apart from Him, our lives are earthbound and futile.

The maiden has begun to recognize this as she exclaims, **"Do not stare at me . . . because I am darkened by the sun."** The sun speaks of the natural realm (life under the sun). Our natural inheritance in Adam left us with a darkened soul. How amazing that God takes this sunburnt maiden and prepares her to be a glorious Bride, transforming her by love. It is time for an identity transplant. Go ahead; ask Jesus how He sees you . . . I dare you!

The Shulamite is ashamed at the discovery of her defects. She now realizes that others are aware of them too. She pleads, "Please . . . don't look at what's wrong with me. You might not like what you see." Self-conscious about her sin; and feeling like everyone is looking at her, she is miserable.

Sound familiar? Have you ever felt like your "sin" is showing? When God exposes us as we are, it is proof that we are growing in our journey.

Be careful not to let shame cause you to be overly introspective and constantly analyzing how you look to others. You were not meant to spend a lifetime with guilt as your companion. Jesus is to be your companion. You really are His beloved one, His favorite. There is a vast difference between knowing you are forgiven and knowing you are His favorite.

Jesus, the Redeemer, is your Bridegroom. Let His Words fill your heart! Our performance is not our meditation, He is our meditation! And neither are the words of those who use us for their own ends . . .

The Angry Brothers

Who are **"my mother's sons?"** Her brothers . . . her brothers that are angry with her. The Crisis of Rejection has come! Her youthful zeal to pursue Jesus wholeheartedly arouses the jealous anger of her brethren. There will be a time when your zeal for the Father's house will provoke others (Ps. 69:8-9). Often our zeal is without maturity, and we do silly things that cause others to reject us—yet even this is a test. The angry brothers take full advantage of her zeal and fervency. They overwork her in their fields. She becomes the keeper of *their* vineyards while her own vineyard is overgrown with weeds. She has not had time to make herself desirable for her Lover . . . she has been busy and overburdened with everyone's expectations.

How easily we can be driven by a need for approval from others rather than our need for fellowship with Him! Anger, jealousy, and hard words are all a part of the old order of church life. God's true servants do not strive or speak harshly to those "keeping watch" over the flock. How often we are expected to keep others' goats!

Taking responsibilities apart from God's grace is a recipe for burnout. Overworked laborers in God's vineyards will be discouraged, and sometimes quit. Weariness takes our joy and makes us feel guilty we are not doing more for God. All of this becomes a religious yoke, which in time proves to be heavy on our shoulders.

Christ's yoke is easy and light. He is coupled to us— united to us in the yoke of love. A yoke of religious responsibilities given to us by overworked leaders will take us out of the will of God. As we are newly awakened to fervency, we become vulnerable to the false yokes of the church. When we find our identity in what *we do* for God, instead of *intimacy with Christ*, we can lose our vision.

The vineyard of others drained her spiritual life, leaving her own vineyard (her own inner life in God) neglected. Your life in the Spirit is a vineyard, a garden for the Lord. To neglect your own vineyard is to abandon your call to pursue Jesus with an undistracted love. Cultivating the garden-heart is a daily responsibility.

It is the strategy of the devil to sidetrack you from your pure devotion to God. If he can keep you exhausted and overloaded with a religious yoke, he knows that in time, your life of intimacy with Jesus will suffer.

Others will try to tell you that you can't afford to take the time to be alone with God. Like Martha they will expect you to cook dinner. They may even misunderstand that you are being drawn into a life of passionate pursuit of God; yet all of this only refines our motives. The day will come when our own vineyard (inner life) will be refreshing and our labors for God will not be to impress people, but will become the overflow of His life in us. He will become our very great Reward.

"Tell me, You whom I love. . . ." She realizes now that it is not the church or others; it is Him whom she loves! She must have Him. She says three times in this passage, "You." Regardless of the cost, she wants the fellowship of this King continually.

"Tell me . . . where you graze your flock and where you rest your sheep at midday." She wants to know where He leads His flock at noon when the sun is the brightest. Midday is a season of light and glory. She longs to be in the midday brightness with her shepherd. She is saying, "I have been fed by others but I am still empty. My hunger is for You, not just teachings about You. Bring me into Your midday light of revelation, untroubled by darkness. Take me there. I am weary with *doing stuff* (keeping vineyards). Now I want to rest in Your shadow. Where do you rest your sheep? Take me *there.*"

The exquisite love of Jesus is a fountain that will never dry up. You can drink your fill. This is where Jesus rests His flock at midday . . . at His fountain of delight. Now she sees this King as a Shepherd—a gentle, satisfying Shepherd.

What a fitting name for Jesus: *"The Lord is my Shepherd"* (Ps. 23:1). He will lead His flock into the perfect pasture, the *"green"* pasture where we will grow the most. The pasture for you is measured according to the hunger that you possess. The Shulamite must be fed directly from the heart of her Shepherd; resting under the midday glory. She is ready to feed her own soul with Him (Matt. 11:28-29).

"Why should I be like a veiled woman beside the flocks of your friends?" The Hebrew text is "a wandering woman." She asks the Shepherd why she should continue to be like a veiled woman wandering in shame. Her cry is for Him to take away her shame (Isa. 4:1). You and I must have an unveiled face before the Lord. Shame is a veil that will keep us from seeing clearly. When we are ashamed, our gaze is on ourself, our failures. It is time to lift the veil and gaze on Him undistracted. Only the Shepherd can remove the veil of shame from the human heart, not just His friends (fivefold ministries). The maiden's willingness to serve has been used by others.

She has been busy keeping the vineyards of her brothers, now she wants to find her Beloved. Even though her own vineyard (devotional life) has not been maintained, she still knows that He is the One she loves. She is consumed with a desperate hunger even in her weakness. . . . But where can she find Him? His answer will surprise her. . . .

The tender Shepherd is compassionate in her weakness (James 5:11). Others would have rebuked her for being too busy, too distracted. The first words He speaks in this Song of Songs is to call the immature maiden the **"most beautiful of women."** There is none more kind and gentle than He.

Our Lord instructs His prophet to speak tenderly to Jerusalem and tell her that her hard service is over (Isa. 40:1). True prophetic ministry is the voice of Jesus speaking to His Bride, the testimony He wants to speak over us (Rev. 19:10). He is infinitely kind to those who fail. The bruises of life are healed by His touch (word). That the King would call this goat-smelling, sun-darkened maiden the loveliest of women is simply unbelievable. He describes His Bride-to-be as "beautiful" although she could only see herself darkened by sin, even while she is feeling distant from Him.

Who is the fairest of them all? Why . . . *you are* in His sight! Is this how you see yourself? Let Jesus speak right into your shame, your busyness, your rejection . . . hear Him tell you how fair you are to Him. Cherish His love. We often look for mental answers. We want to figure it out, but God simply wants to touch our hearts. If we "figure it out" then we will always relate to God by our minds. Your King wants you to know Him in your *heart*, with the fullness of your *passion*. Love created you out of Love, to share Love with you. . . .

The Shulamite's cry for the Shepherd made her beautiful in His sight. Jesus does not just see the sinful struggle; He sees the seeking heart! He does not define us by the unkept vineyard we display but by the budding virtues yet to grow into fullness. How kind is your Shepherd! You are safe with a Friend like this One.

"If you do not know . . . " It is so important we know that we are lovely in His sight. The power of hope is released when we drink of these words. If we do not know, we will not grow! Knowing we are loved while unworthy builds a fortress around our souls. Doubt, fear, and accusation cannot take root in us.

When we are tempted to quit out of self-disgust and condemnation, it is this revelation that redeems us: 'I call you Most Beautiful because you seek me even in your weakness.' The great secret of your heart that God will someday reveal is not your sin, but your fervent love for Him that would not give up in your search for Him (I Cor. 4:5).

"Follow the tracks of the sheep"

He gives her three unexpected answers to her request for intimacy. *First,* He instructs her to follow the footsteps of the flock. "You will not find me in the busy streets of the world but follow the flock of those who hear His voice" (John 10:27-28).

At times we lose our way . . . we need examples to follow. She needs direction. She needs an answer. . . . What will He tell her?

It is time to get involved with the Body. She cannot draw back from "Body-Life" just because the angry brothers wounded her. If she is to find the Shepherd's resting place, she must reconnect to the flock He leads. The devil wants us in isolation. If he cannot overwork us with premature responsibilities, he will keep us isolated and wounded. Overreacting to all the religious yokes of the church will cause many to hide in their caves, disillusioned with church and church leaders.

The wise Shepherd encourages her to reconnect with a flock that follows Him. Others are in pursuit of Him — get in step with them and move on. Simply stated: Jesus wants you to stay committed to the Body of Christ. The woundings of your heart are your tests to mature your faith. If you have been hurt on the "killing fields" of the church, you must move on with His flock, regardless of how you were treated in the past. When the "angry" brothers mistreat us, our temptation is to leave the church and isolate ourselves. "Lord, I only want You! I will never let anyone hurt me again."

Sadly, many in the church today have made inner vows never to be open again to others, especially spiritual leaders. These inner vows must someday be broken, making us vulnerable again. We find the Shepherd with His sheep—His *corporate* Bride, not just individuals. So often we will only find the Shepherd when we are in sweet fellowship with His people.

She cries out for His kisses (1:2), but where do you find His kisses? Christ lives in every believer as much as He lived in His mother's house on earth. Jesus is the only person who has two bodies: one, as the Son of Man who lived two thousand years ago and is now seated in heaven; and another which is the Body He now has on earth, His church.

We can kiss Him when we kiss our brethren. In the same way, we can receive His kisses through our brothers and sisters. These are the "holy kisses" we are to give to others. Every time we love a brother or sister like Jesus does, we have planted on them a "holy kiss," the very kiss of Jesus through His church (Rom. 16:16)!

Jesus said, *"Blessed are those who are pure in heart: for they will see God."* We can see God in one another when our hearts are washed in Calvary's love. Those who sentenced Stephen to death (Acts 6) saw the face of the martyr as though it were the face of an angel. They could see an angel in their victim.

Perhaps we should look at others the way they saw Stephen. Then we would be able to receive "holy kisses" (Rom. 16:16). Paul was speaking of more than making sure that our kisses are not sensual; He was referring to the Holy Kisses of the Song of Solomon.

We, as His Body, can give the Holy Kiss as we love others in their weaknesses. When we bless others (kiss them in His love), such as giving drink to the thirsty (those needing His love), and when we take in the stranger (loving those who are not like us), we are actually offering our love to Jesus Himself (Matt. 25:35-40).

Take Care of Responsibilities

The Shepherd gives His *second* reply to her request for greater intimacy. She must take care of the things God has given her. She is told only to feed those little goats that are under her care. Don't do *everything* in the church; just take care of the responsibilities *God* has given you.

In the past she took on too many things, the responsibilities of her angry brothers. Now she is free to graze her young goats. She could easily say, "But Lord, this is how it started last time. I got burned out taking on too many things. I am too weary to feed others, just let me soak awhile." He tells her, *and He tells us—*"You will find Me when you give yourself to bless and feed others. Take your undisciplined affections and graze them on Me!" She must recommit to serve again. This is difficult if you have once been "burned out" by serving. . . . It is the last thing you want to hear! Yet Father knows best.

Stay Connected to Those Who Love Him

There is an ancient proverb that says, "If you wish to smell pleasant, stand near those who sell perfume." You will find the Lord near the "tents" of godly leaders. This is His *third* reply to her request for greater intimacy—stay connected to those closest to the Bridegroom. Those who are in pursuit of Jesus must have an open spirit to their leaders. "But Lord, don't you know that Your leaders are imperfect? They wounded once, must I be vulnerable again?" The Lord answers with, "Yes, for this is how I have designed you to grow up into my image." As we discover the grace to relate to imperfect shepherds, we discover Him in deeper ways. God is the One who chooses His shepherds. They are the ones that will lead us to Him! It is important that we draw life from others who follow our King. If we have a "know-it-all" attitude and remain unteachable, we will miss the One we are looking for.

Her cry for kisses, her longing to be drawn into the King's chambers of intimacy has brought her forward in her journey. The first crisis has come with the pressure and pain of her inadequacy. So far she has had to experience the following:

+ The sense of shame over her "dark" ways and human failure.
+ The "angry brothers" have rejected her.
+ She is overworked with religious duties.
+ Distraction caused her garden-heart to be full of weeds.
+ Jesus seems to be distant. Her service is without intimacy.

The Lord of Love knows just what fuel we need in our tank to see us through the difficult times of disorientation and failure. He knows all the pressure she is enduring and still He calls her beautiful. How He loves His Bride . . .

She doesn't know it yet, but every time He comes with words of affirmation and tenderness, it is to prepare her for a further test. The preparation we need is found in His caresses.

Our healing will be in a relationship, not just an anointed meeting. He is about to give her a "fill up" at His service station of grace . . . full service!

---

[1] The word for dark means "scorched, or darkened by the sun." Solomon says that life "under the sun" is vanity and will 'scorch' our soul.

[2] The Hebrew word for lovely can also mean "graceful, loveable, desirable."

[3] *Kedar* means "a dark chamber." Kedar was also a son of Ishmael, who is a type of the flesh.

[4] Fine linen in the Bible speaks of righteousness (Rev. 19:8).

The Kind Shepherd

Chapter 1:9-15
ꝏCʒ

*J*esus comes to her as the Most Kind Shepherd. This is how we also find Him when we ask Him into our lives . . . so gentle, pleasing, and compassionate. He is all that and more — much more. In this season of life, the maiden is pleased with how He satisfies her; how deeply His Words touch her! But she hasn't a clue as to what lies ahead . . . only that He is with her, and she is happy to have Him at her side.

Once again He sings this sublime song of love to her heart. With supreme tenderness He speaks to her every time with words like, *"My Darling," "Most Beautiful,"* or *"My Beloved."* This shows the heart of God toward us even while we are immature. Weak people touch the heart of God. His affection toward us is beyond our understanding.

The word **"darling"** is literally, "Lover-Friend." You have the privilege of becoming the "lover-friend" of the Son of God. Every time He looks at you He is thrilled with your seeking heart. Let no one take this truth from you! Think about it. Jesus calls you darling. He is tender beyond words . . . kind to us, when we still feel ugly and sinful. No one on earth speaks this way to us when we fail. These Divine "kisses" are what will sustain her in the wilderness . . . just like they sustain us in ours. . . .

The apostle Luke wrote two books in the New Testament, Luke and Acts. They were addressed to one named Theophilus, which means, "lover of God." Beloved, it is doubtful there was a man named Theophilus that received Luke and Acts as a letter. . . . They were written to you, "most excellent *lover of God*" (Luke. 1:1-4, Acts 1:1).

You must begin to place your name over the writings of the Bible and realize that it was all written as a love letter to you, the fiancée of Jesus Christ! Too many of us are working frantically to earn the right to stay in His kingdom. We need to rest in knowing that we are His darling, His favorite one. Look at it this way, if God had a wallet . . . your picture would be in it!

"I liken you, my darling, to a mare harnessed to one of the chariots of Pharaoh." He calls her a filly, a mare! Is this a compliment? How would you like to be called a horse? What does He mean by this? Could it be that her strong desire to follow Him is like the strength of the finest horse pulling a king's chariot? In ancient poetry the horse was always used as an emblem of beauty and inner strength. Her strong passion to know Him is like the strength of a racehorse pulling Pharaoh's chariot!

Historians write of the chariot of Pharaoh. It was embossed with pure gold, so that when the sun shone upon it, its glare would blind the armies of the enemy. The royal, golden chariot was only drawn by the most beautiful of horses. Jesus is saying to you, "Let me tell you what I think of you. Your brave desire to follow Me is beautiful in my sight. Your elegant strength to do righteousness is much more intense than you realize. I see your hidden potential. . . . You may feel like a failure, but I see you as the strong mare harnessed to my heart."

Jesus is saying to you: "You're the best there is! You have been trained like Pharaoh's horses to carry the King Himself. You are not offensive to Me. . . . You are beautiful to Me! You are as swift and as strong as a racehorse to run after Me." You see, Jesus holds a crown over your head and lets you grow up into it. . . .

He Describes Her Emotions Toward Him

"Your cheeks are beautiful." The cheeks, or "countenance," speak of our emotions. You reveal your emotions by your countenance. Anger, joy, sadness, and shame are always seen on the cheeks, for this is where we express what is inside of us. When He calls her cheeks beautiful, He acknowledges her tender emotions towards Him. He is delighted with her! Did you know that your emotions are attractive to God?

The Lord designed you to be emotional. Jesus made us to have emotions that He could fill and direct towards His heart. A denial of our emotions is a denial of who we were made to be. Jesus touches our emotions by His Spirit. This is how He made us . . . how we were made to work! This King has touched her emotional make-up. He sees her fervency toward Him and calls it beautiful. You may think others are strange when they show their emotions toward Jesus but He calls it beautiful. She cries out "Draw me" (1:4) and He draws her heart toward Himself.

"Beautiful with earrings." Jesus is the artist, the craftsman of every heart. He adorns us in His grace to be beautiful in His sight (Isa. 61:3). He is telling her: "You look good and I like you!"

These earrings are the grace gifts that He has placed upon us that we might have beauty before Him. You are gorgeous to Him! *"The King is enthralled by your beauty"*

(Ps. 45:11). He loves to make His Bride beautiful by giving her ears to hear His voice, and a heart to respond.

Jesus loves it when you are alone with Him. When you are not attached to other things, you become attached to Him. It is time to find time to be with the One who calls you beautiful.

He Sees Her Yielded Will

"Your neck with strings of jewels . . ." The neck speaks of the will. We can be "stiff-necked" (a sign of a stubborn will) or we can bow the neck (a sign of submission, reverent). The neck is what turns the head and directs the body. Our will is what chooses the path we go on. The King calls her neck lovely because she has submitted her will to follow Him.

The jewels on her neck speak of royalty, authority. She has said "yes" to God and is resolute to follow this King. When Jesus looks upon you He sees the "yes" in your spirit, even though you may have seasons of failure. He sees your will submitted to learn the lessons of growing in God. Every time you say Yes to Him, another jewel, or pearl is added to your authority. He sees you as one who has acquired a gentleness to submit to Him, making you lovely.

The Trinity is involved in maturing a Bride for Jesus. Father, Son & Holy Spirit are speaking, **"We will make you earrings of gold, studded with silver."** Gold in the Scriptures points to the Divine character. The day will come when the maiden will be Christ-like, made in the image of His golden character. This is the grace-work of God. He makes us like gold as we continue in our journey in the grace of God. The heart of an extravagant worshipper of Jesus is like refined gold. He promises her that where she lacks, He will supply. He promises to complete the work of refining her heart.

It is Jesus' responsibility to make you shine like gold! God promises to work on you if you will not give up. You are only a failure in life if you quit. Everyone fails, but will you be one who moves on until His gold is found in you?

These "earrings of gold" will impart golden hearing. Tokens of truth will be inserted in our inward ears to know the voice of our Shepherd. Spiritual images and the words of divine wisdom will be whispered to the Bride, for she wears heaven's earrings. . . .

Silver speaks of redemption. Her destiny will be redeemed. Her purpose for existence will take on its full meaning. She will be used to bring redemption to others. Could this "stud of silver" be the Cross of Christ? The Cross is the stud of silver that brings true redemption to our hearts. . . .

Now it's time for her to see the King's Table. . . .

"While the King was at His table . . . " She begins to receive revelation of the King's wealth and provisions. A new understanding begins to fill her. The full provision of salvation starts to dawn on her; "He is more than a Shepherd, He is a King! He is a glorious King with wealth and splendor beyond comprehension." She is taken to His Table to see all that He provides for His household. What a table He has spread for *you!*

Just think . . . Jesus wants to dine with you.

Have you ever thought of how much food a king would have at his table? Take a look at I Kings 4:22-27. . . . It describes the abundance of a king's table. One hundred and eighty-five bushels of fine flour were used to make the bread for one day! Ten head of stall-fed cattle, and twenty head of pasture-fed cattle were consumed each day at Solomon's table! *"Sheep, goats, deer, gazelles, roe-*

bucks, and choice fowl" were prepared for just one day's provision. What abundance the king served! Would the King of Kings have any less?

O, the wonderful provisions of the Cross of Christ! How much He has given us by the Blood of His Cross! You were given more than you can imagine on the day you said "yes" and became His child.

This Shulamite shepherdess now begins to understand how awesome is her Tender King. He fed her spirit on the revelation of who He is and what He has done for her. She asked in 1:7, "Where would you feed me?" Now she begins to understand — at His table!

When we forget the open invitation to the King's table, our spirit starves. We begin to feed our soul on the "husks" of this world. Why would we wander when there is abundance at the King's table? Every spiritual blessing has been given to us at this Table (Eph. 1:3). Beloved, you married into great wealth. . . .

This Shepherd-King will feed us even in the presence of our enemies. Even in the midst of personal struggles and defeats, there is a feast prepared; the feast of Revelation 3:20. The King wants to dine with us and share the glories of His provisions for us. If only we open the door, He will come in to satisfy our souls.

The "table" was a place of rest and refreshment. It is where we recline and dine, enjoying His love. This couch-table can satisfy us as we lean upon Him and praise Him for His love. Bible scholars for centuries have noted the seven resting places of Jesus:

+ The eternal bosom of the Father.
+ The womb of Mary.
+ The manger outside Bethlehem.
+ The table where He rested and dined with His friends.

- The cross became a place of rest, bowing His head in death.
- The tomb of Joseph of Arimathea.
- The throne He sits upon at the right hand of the Father.

To these seven we may add the eighth . . . The resting place of *the heart of His mystical Bride.* The heart of the Bride becomes the beautiful dwelling place of Yahweh (Ps. 84:1). The heart of one who loves the Lord Jesus is more precious to God than the Temple of Solomon. *You* are now His resting place (Isa. 66:1-2).

Her Spontaneous Worship

"My perfume spread its fragrance." Her perfume (spikenard) begins to spread its fragrance when she sees the King at His table. Spontaneous worship begins to fill the room, as the revelation of the Cross expands her heart. This is a King beyond belief. His abundance releases praise as adoration ascends from her heart to God.[1] Her thoughts are, "How can I honor and treat Him in a way worthy of His love?" Forgetting about herself, her praise-perfume spreads throughout His dining room.

To receive and enjoy all that God provides for you is the key to worship. You have perfume to share with your King. You can bring enjoyment to the heart of Jesus as He receives your praise. Jesus enjoys your aroma as you gaze on Him in worship. Your perfume ascends to God like incense before the altar of heaven (Rev. 5:8).

The Corinthian church was the most carnal (fleshly) in the New Testament. It was to them that Paul wrote: "We are to God the aroma of Christ . . . " (II Cor. 2:15). Immature saints that worship even out of their brokenness release the sweetest perfume into heaven . . . the fragrance of Christ. The virtues of Jesus come forth as we worship God.

In Luke 7, the prostitute poured out spikenard upon the feet of our Lord This was her act of worshipping the Son of God out of her brokenness. The spiritual perfume she released thrilled the heart of Jesus as He witnessed her devotion with kisses and tears.

Those who have been forgiven much, worship much. Have you been forgiven much? Can you worship Him right where you are in a place of brokenness?

Her Meditation of the Cross

"My Lover is to me a sachet of myrrh. . . . " As she praises the King at His table of abundance the maiden begins to smell something. . . . It smells sweet but pungent. Is it her spikenard? No, it is myrrh. Her perfume has been completely overwhelmed by the fragrance of myrrh. She smells the sufferings of Christ.

Myrrh is an expensive perfume used by the wealthy as a burial spice. Jacob sent myrrh down to Egypt as one of the choice and costly products of the land. The wise kings who visited Jesus presented gold, frankincense, and myrrh as a prophetic sign. Embalming spice was given to Jesus at His birth! Myrrh is also a symbol of His death, His Cross. It was mixed with wine and offered to Jesus on the cross. When Mary came to the tomb of Jesus she brought with her myrrh.

But there is no amount of myrrh that could be compared to the costly sacrifice of Jesus on the Tree! All of His garments smell of myrrh (Ps. 45:8). The Hebrew word for myrrh is a form of the word, "bitter." The ancient Hebrews describe myrrh as, "tears from a tree." It is from the Sacred Tree that liquid love pours down, whispering — "It is finished."

The cross is a bundle of *myrrh*. As the maiden first catches the scent of myrrh, she begins to understand what following the King will cost her. What if following Him brings pain and sacrifice? What if it will mean rejection and misunderstanding and dying to our own strength?

But every Shulamite cries out, "He is worth it! My Lover is to me a sachet of myrrh resting between my breasts." The maiden reveals her "Bridal spirit" by her willingness to follow Jesus at all costs. The dimensions of His leadership have penetrated her inwardly. She will embrace Him to her heart[2] as a bundle of myrrh.

A bundle is something tied up and bound. Jesus was tied up and nailed to the cross as a bundle of myrrh for you. A bundle of lovely virtues is our Lord Jesus! He is a marvelous variety of Prophet, Priest, King, Husband, Shepherd, and Friend. We take the bundle of His virtue into our hearts; His gentleness, courage, compassion, strength, and unfailing kindness. His suffering love is like the fragrance of myrrh.

The cross will make you beautiful . . . sweet smelling. As we draw near to the place of sacrifice and adore the One who gave it all away to save the world . . . this is what releases the scent of myrrh upon us. Others will recognize that you have been with Him. The smell of myrrh is upon you when you lay down your life for others. . . .

Other translations read, "Like a bundle of myrrh that lies all night between my breasts." She gives constant meditation to the cross; it is not a passing doctrine on her way to something else. Through all the seasons of our lives we give ourselves to a deeper revelation of His Cross. If you spend time at His table you will see His cross and smell His myrrh. You will begin to understand the price He paid to draw you to Himself. He became a bouquet or sachet of myrrh for you! If meditation on the cross seems boring to you, it is only because you do not understand it. Paul's only boast was in the Cross of our Lord Jesus (Gal. 6:14).

It is simply amazing that the God who created everything became a Man. The angels must be amazed before this mystery. Yet, even more amazing to men and angels was that the God-Man died on a tree. These sacred mysteries unlock the heart of the Father and the essence of eternity. All throughout earth's "night" we do well to meditate on the glories of the Cross.

To contemplate the cross is the gateway to God. The mysteries of the birth and childhood of Jesus, His baptism by His prophetic cousin John, the open heavens and the despairing desert, the trials of His ministry, the exhaustion of His journeys, His prayers, His fasts, His tears and compassion for the rebellious, the deceits of His enemies, the accusations, the jeers and insults, the beatings and the bruises, the nails . . . the thorns. . . .

All of these become the mysterious myrrh of His sufferings. On your way to the Blessed Tree, stop and meditate on the sufferings of Jesus that restored life to you. Drink it in; it is a deep cup of love for the thirsty.

My Lover is to ME. . . . Dear one, is Jesus *your* Lover? Is He like a bundle of fragrant myrrh to *you*? Do you love Him with a raging love? Is your religion only in your head, never reaching deep into your heart? To many, He is boring and irrelevant; but what is He to *you*? Our deepest pleasure, our purest joy is found in Him. . . .

She Proclaims His Beauty

"My Lover is to me a cluster of henna blossoms . . . "
Jesus is the loveliest flower filled with sweet fragrance. His beauty captivates our souls. The maiden discovers, after meditation on the Cross, how lovely is this King. Even His sufferings become sweetness and delightful to

every tender heart. When we see by inward revelation how beautiful He is, we can never go on the way we were; we become lovers of God—longing for His beauty.

The Hebrew word for henna is *"kopher,"* which is also translated "atonement." Jewish teachers in ancient times believed the phrase "a cluster of henna blossoms" was a reference to the Messiah. They translated it, 'a man who atones for all.'

The fragrance of Christ's atonement for all our sins is a sweet fragrance indeed. Why doesn't the world see His beauty? He is not a burdensome, heavy-handed King. He is not the religious god of the Pharisees. . . . He is the Prince of Life; the Splendor and Glory of God. With fresh revelation we must convey to others that He is our Dream come true.

There is One who is so altogether lovely, so incredibly faithful and true, that your heart is safe in His care. He is not just a flower, but a **"cluster"** of flowers! His beauty comes from every aspect of His character. You could never take it all in. He is a cluster of beauty before our heart. Have you ever found another who is so tender with our weaknesses? He understands our failures completely, yet passionately embraces us anyway!

In these early stages of spiritual growth we notice the focus is what He is to the maiden, not what she is to Him. As the story progresses, this will change. But for now, she is caught up with His beauty, and her right to enjoy Him. Later, she must realize that He has rights to enjoy her!

Her one theme now is that this wonderful King loves her. The day will come in *your* life when you will know that He has total ownership of your heart. You exist for Him alone, without consideration of your comforts and pleasures. With a focus entirely on Him, you will see yourself as His desired one, His beloved. What a "love-theology!" Soon the Shulamite will understand more fully what that means. . . .

His Divine Affection

"**How beautiful you are, my darling . . .** " Words like these wash over our souls. When we understand who is saying it, our minds cannot comprehend it. Jesus, the radiant Son, calls you beautiful. He calls you His darling . . . His fair one, His true friend. He affirms the maiden in her new worship, her new revelation of the Cross. He responds to her with the affirmation of Divine affection: "**How beautiful you are.**" **Jesus doesn't just say, "You look beautiful" . . . He says, "You ARE beautiful!"**

Most of us, if we are honest, do not see ourselves as very lovable. What does Jesus see in us? Why would He call *me* beautiful? A radical love like this cannot be explained — it can only be enjoyed! Who can explain the power of a lover's kiss? There are things in God that are not meant to be understood; they are to be received by faith and cherished. He has given us all things (including the revelation of His love) to be enjoyed (I Tim. 6:17). We see this revelation poetically portrayed in the Song of Songs. Beloved, it will take forever for the mind to catch up with what God has put in our spirits.

Believers sometimes say that the church is ugly, messed up . . . full of problems. Others could look at you or I and say the same thing. Many Christians look at how God loves and blesses those they struggle with . . . so they pray:

"Lord...don't you see how much so-and-so has hurt me?
Don't you see how bad they are, how immature,
how messed up they are?"

Jesus looks beyond the momentary mess to see into the motives of our hearts. The longing of the Bride is for Him. This is what thrills His heart and causes Him to tell her again how beautiful she is. God can look at the very people you see as ugly and call them beautiful. Where you see blemishes, He sees beauty.

Jesus is determined to leap over the mountains of fear and jump over our walls of insecurity until He has fully captured our hearts in love. When this grips us, we will no longer strive to make God like us, winning His approval with good behavior.

Knowing how God sees you is the one true healing balm of the wounded heart. Everything else, every program and therapy, is only a "Band-Aid." God's love heals. It casts out fear and brings in confidence. His deep affection removes loneliness and rejection from your heart. His overwhelming love overcomes our insecurities and makes us whole again. This must be learned at the beginning of our journey with Christ, or we will stumble all along the way.

Too often we interpret His discipline as anger, not love. We think He is rejecting us when He is actually correcting us. We carry wounds in our hearts, seeing ourselves as ugly, mistreated, and unloved throughout life. Unable to receive His love deep inside, we are not able to give love to others. All our lives we seek the love of others and feel that we need them to survive, when it is only HIS love, which brings true satisfaction and healing.

A sense of rejection follows us because we were born in sin, lost "in Adam." But the healing love of Jesus comes when we understand that we are born *again* in Christ Jesus, who calls us beautiful even while we are immature! Jesus cherishes you because you said "yes" to Him. Not because you are perfect, but because your fear was conquered by His love.

This is what releases power to our inner man to over-come bondage, and cast out the darkness of our souls. Running after Him in bridal affection is the key to per-sonal deliverance. Becoming incurably devoted to the One who gave sacred blood for you—this will redeem your days! Can you see the Lord looking down on you full of admiration saying:

> *O, I love you. I find delight in you—you fill me with such pleasure! My heart swells with joy each time I think of you; each time I call your name! I see the sin-cerity of your devotion to Me. I look inside of you and see the desire you have to be Mine. Listen to Me child— I call you lovely!*

Jesus repeats it for impact: **"How beautiful!"** He seems to momentarily forget His greatness to speak to His Beloved Bride, twice calling her beautiful. Once is not enough for Him! Once is not enough for us! He gives the maiden an ever-fresh proclamation of His tender love. Over and over He will tell us . . . Yet we never grow weary of hearing His adoring words.

Dove-Eyes

The King has heard her worship, her meditation. He has noticed her beauty. Now He locks eyes with hers and says, **"Your eyes are doves."** He sees in her a beautiful creature who can fly into His heart and abide there forev-er. The One who has the Spirit without measure is able to see this same Spirit life in His Bride. Who is it that made her eyes like doves if not Him? Love makes what is uniquely His available to her.

The eyes speak of the ability to see spiritual truths. She is growing in her perception of who He is. With eyes of faith and clear spiritual vision, she is starting to see how awesome this King really is.

We are told that the eyes of a dove are only able to focus on one thing at a time. He sees that she is looking only to Him (Matt. 6:22). She has become single-minded in grace, not tossed about by condemnation and rejection. Her emotional tank is being filled with His love. She is able to see clearly all that He has done for her, as her focus turns to Him alone. Her eyes search for the source of fire that passes through her when He looks at her.

She trusts Him . . . at least she trusts Him as far as she knows Him. She is learning much, but the great revelation of who He really is awaits her on the mountaintops. . . . But is she willing to go? Does she trust Him enough to go to the mountains of myrrh?

---

[1] It was while Jesus and His friends were "reclining at the table" that Mary, the extravagant lover, poured out her expensive spikenard upon His feet. . . .

[2] The maiden is saying the revelation of the cross is like a bundle of myrrh that lies between her breasts, not on her *shoulders*. He is no heavy burden, but a joy to the heart.

His Banner of Love

Chapter 1:16-2:7
೧೦೮೫

$\mathcal{T}$his is a wonderful season in the maiden's life. She is seeing this Shepherd-King as the one who is feeding her apples, unfurling His banner, embracing her in His arms. Life just doesn't get much better than this. When the Lord comes to you with waves of refreshing, receive it. Drink in the wine of His love. . . . You will need it for the lessons He has in store for you . . . those unexpected lessons He is preparing you to learn. Listen to her response:

"How handsome you are, my Lover!" The more He speaks words of love, the more glorious He becomes in her eyes. Love releases revelation to our hearts. With an unguarded spirit, our hearts open. We begin to take notice of who this loving King is. As she is washed by love, what will her response be to this revelation? She adores Jesus more than ever!

The key to growing in God is receiving the revelation of His love (Eph. 3:18). The fourfold dimension of this love brings the fullness of Jesus into our lives. We will never grow in God apart from a context of being enjoyed by Him. Worship must flow from a heart captured by this love. The loveliness of the King penetrates the Shulamite's spirit. Jesus is becoming more and more attractive to her.

He is not the harsh, driving master that she imagined Him to be. Religious lies told her to keep her guard up, to cringe when she came near Him. But now she discovers His glorious tenderness, even in her immaturity and weakness.

Jesus satisfies. No one is as kind as He. It is nothing but a lie that keeps others away from Him! There is never unkindness or harshness with Him. His commands are not burdensome; they are life-giving! Every feature about this Prince is glorious. The bride-to-be is making a new discovery of how trustworthy He is to her. There is an exchange of deep affection between the two of them at this moment. As they lock eyes with each other a love that lasts a lifetime is birthed.

When Jesus appears handsome to *your* soul, when *you* see His lovely face, when the kindness of His brow pierces *your* heart, wholehearted obedience to Him becomes reasonable. It is so right to fall in love with Him. It is so right to go anywhere He sends you. It is so right to give up all other pursuits to follow Him! When we expect and deserve a lecture, He stoops to kiss us. When we fully expect the clenched fist, He opens His palm to show us the nail scar. What a charming King He is! Who would not love Him?

"Our bed is verdant . . . " You have been seated with Christ in heavenly places... there is no better resting place than this (Eph. 2:6). The maiden has the revelation of the luxurious restingplace given to her by the King. He has made her lie down in green (verdant) pastures. Verdant in the Hebrew speaks of abundance and luxury. She rests in the presence of God, because of the abundance of His love. She speaks of *"Our bed;"* she sees the truth of being a co-heir with Him! The cross has now become her resting place. In the sanctuary of His sweet heart we rest and abide. What a soft, safe bed is the Bridegroom's heart.

The King has shown her the "green room" in His palace . . . the place of growth, maturity, and rest. This room shall be ours forever! As the Shulamite looks around the room, she glances up.

"The beams of our house are cedars . . . " Cedar is a hard wood. As she journeys toward life union with this King, strength and safety are all around the Shulamite maiden. She sees the security of *"our house"* and rests safely with Him. The cedar tree is an emblem of life and the cypress or fir is a symbol of death.[1] Both of these are the two major building materials in Solomon's Temple. They speak of the life and death of our Lord Jesus that has become our security and covering.

"Our rafters are firs." The word "rafters" literally means "galleries" or "balconies." These are the porches, which extend out from the house . . . the enclosed deck. The bride and bridegroom sit and walk together in sweet fellowship on a balcony made of fir, a fragrant and durable wood.

The house is the church, The House of the Lord (I Tim. 3:15). She is now ready to enter back into fellowship with others. She understands that He is her resting place and security. Her heart has been overwhelmed with His expressions of love. Now she must face new tests and grow in her journey towards Christ-likeness. . . . But first, she must embrace her true identity.

Her Understanding Grows

"I am a rose of Sharon . . . " Scholars are split over who is speaking; the King or the maiden. I believe it is the maiden here who confesses her identity in Jesus; she calls herself a rose of Sharon. Beloved, you are His rosebud!
The Father has given a rose to His Son. The Bride of Christ must see herself as His Rose. The riches of redemption have been freely given, the robe of righteousness is upon us — we are a Rose of Sharon.

As she calls herself **"a rose,"** the maiden is beginning to see herself as His inheritance; one who brings pleasure and enjoyment to His heart. She is the inheritance that the Father promised to give to His Son. You too, are God's love gift to Jesus.

It is time for you to see yourself as a Rose of Sharon—the great prize promised to Jesus. Sharon means, *"His song."* The maiden suddenly realizes that she is the theme (rose) of His Song! The singing King has plucked His rose-bud and held it to His heart.

It is time to no longer see yourself as unworthy of His love . . . but as a rose that intoxicates the heart of our Lord. You are the theme of His Song, His rose of Sharon!

The Father cultivated this Rose for His Son. With tender care, the God of heaven caused the rose to grow and open its blossom to the love of the Son. This Rose represents the fullness of everything Jesus desires. You have fully won His heart!

When you understand that you are the Rose of Sharon, difficulties don't matter; for there is an Anchor of hope that holds you. When you are overwhelmed in your weakness, you are still His rosebud. The Rose of Christ is now our identity. The end-time church will soon confess that we are His rose. Like a Rose that has blossomed in the wilderness, the Bride will see herself as the cherished of His heart (Isa. 35:1-2).

Her *"Lily White"* Spirit

"A lily of the valley. . . . " In Hosea 14:5 the prophet calls God's people a lily. In the deepest valleys of our lives we are still united to Jesus Christ. Our love for Him cannot be taken from us in the valley, for He sees us as His lily. Lilies speak of purity. As Jesus' lovely lily, the maiden-bride acknowledges that she is pure in His sight. *You* are the one lily that sparkles with dew in the eyes of Jesus the Bridegroom. This is true even in the low and dark places of life. Your whole life can be redefined when you claim this as your identity; **"I am a rose of Sharon, a lily of the valley."**

The bride of Christ still has much to learn. She is still immature and self-centered. The cross has not fully broken her — but her identity is that of a worshipper and a lover of God. The power of love has connected to her heart. Whatever lies ahead, she knows that He loves her and that she is the delight of His heart. What is the King's reply to her revelation of her identity? He affirms her value and beauty . . . **"Like a lily among thorns is my darling."**

In the midst of a world filled with thorns[2], Jesus calls us His darling lily. Please stop and think about that. You are so precious to Him that He reached His hands into the thorns and held you to Himself. Jesus tore His hands reaching in to rescue you.

Beloved, you are the fiancée of Jesus Christ — there is nothing He would not do for you! Calvary's nails were like thorns ripping His flesh as He had to find you and hold you to Himself. The thorns speak of the curse of sin upon our world (Gen. 3:18). As a fragrant lily she spreads her blessings, even in the midst of the curse. Without striving or toiling, she is arrayed in beauty in this fallen world. Jesus said to His troubled disciples, "Consider the LILIES."

Beloved, listen to His words, **"Like a lily among thorns is my darling among the maidens."** Among the maidens of the earth there is one who longs for purity. In the midst of the curse of this fallen world she longs for Him. She is the Bride of Christ. The King affirms her value. There is no one quite like her. There is no one quite like you! Others have hurt Him, but you have nourished His heart. . . . You are like a lily surrounded by thorns.[3]

Lilies harm no one. . . . Thorns tear and hurt others. Thorns say, "Keep away." The lily says, "Come, I am here to please you."

Jesus sends us out as sheep among wolves, not as sheep among sheep. We are not merely to be lilies in a vase, but lilies among thorns. When we begin to understand this we cry; "But Lord, I am hurt as I walk among the wolves." "Yes child, but you must be my lamb. Just as I clothed Adam and Eve in lambskin, so I send you out as my lamb." A lily will not retaliate.

Beloved, it is the ungodly and hurtful who truly teach us to be His lamb, His lily. Is your influence sweet in this world? Or are you rough and stern like a thorn bush? May we be those who walk as lilies/lambs in the midst of a world of hurt and abuse. Lord, make us charming lilies for You . . . just like you were a Lily among the thorns of this fallen world!

Finding Pleasure in Him

"Like an apple tree . . . is my Lover." Jesus is sweet to the taste, pleasant to the eyes. Jesus Christ is our tree of Life. To know Him is more satisfying than any other relationship. In all of humanity, He is the One who fulfills our deepest longings. Jesus alone supplies the needs of our hearts for He excels them all! At this point the maiden realizes there is no equal on earth to this King. No one could ever take His place. Devoted to Him alone, for He is the Tree of heavenly fruit. What refreshing He brings to her spirit!

An Apple Tree in simple beauty stands,
And waves its juicy treasure gracefully,
Among the barren trees which crowd the wood,
Of lofty form, but destitute of fruit;
So Jesus, midst the fallen sons of men
Bears for my use the fruits of covenant love
And fills my heart with rare delight and rest.

"Like an apple tree among the trees of the forest!"
The other "trees" refer to other men. When Jesus healed
the blind man, his first glimpse of sight was of men walking as *trees*. Jesus alone must fill our vision. Not Paul,
Peter, your favorite prophet, pastor, or teacher. Among
all the finest men stands a Tree . . . one more glorious and
charming than all the rest. His Name is Jesus. He must be
our "Lover" among the young men (gifted ones in the
Body).

The Shulamite has found His voice to be a refreshing
voice of hope like no other. Perhaps your father or mother told you that you were worthless, or an ex-spouse
cursed you with his or her anger. Nevertheless, there is a
tall and stalwart Apple Tree among the sons of men that
excels them all. Over all the barren trees that have tried to
rob you of hope, Jesus is your Tree of life.

"I delight to sit in His shade . . . " How can you
describe the pleasure of His presence? It is a delight to be
near Him, to be safe under His shadow, to rest in shady
grace! It is under this shade tree that the human heart
finds absolute tranquillity. No other resting place gives
you true peace like you experience beneath His shade. . . .
Humbly, we submit our souls to His authority, and our
striving is over.

Under the systems of her angry brothers she found
no rest. Keeping the vineyards of others left her discouraged, wounded . . . weary. Now she dwells in the secret
place of His presence, resting under His Lordship.
Imagine . . . if the shadow of Peter brought healing, what
would dwelling in *His shadow* do for you? It is impossible
to exaggerate how great your eternal Groom really is!
Worship becomes a wonder sitting in His shade.

The Cross is the Tree of Life extending its shade to
the weary. Finding a resting place beneath the Cross kept
the maiden safe and satisfied. She relates to Him on the

basis of His work, not her maturity. Why would you want to relate to God on the basis of *your* victory or *your* maturity? When you have a good week, it is His grace that kept you faithful. When you have a bad week, your unworthiness is not the basis of your relationship with God. Feed your heart under the Apple Tree. Take a nap from striving, until you say, *"I delight to sit in His shade."*

"His fruit is sweet to my taste . . . " To draw from His life is to taste a nectar of sweetness. Nothing compares to the fruit of His character. Paul called it the "Fruit of the Spirit" (Gal. 5:22-23). These introductory experiences of grace have brought true spiritual pleasure to her. She is relating to Jesus under the apple tree receiving all the fruits of His work for her. What can compare to this? Intimacy with Jesus has consumed her. Even a little touch of this will go a long way in growing us up in God. She doesn't stand in *her* shade as she eats, she must dwell in His shade to discover these fruits. He is preparing her to step out of her self-absorbed thinking.

His Banner of Love

"He has taken me to the Banquet Hall . . . " As she sits under the Apple Tree she has a vision. She sees the King taking her into the Banquet Hall. As we delight ourselves in His presence, He invites us even nearer to His heart, into His Banquet Hall. In Chapter One she was taken into the King's chambers, now she is escorted into the Banquet Hall for the engagement party! As the guests enjoy the feast, the King offers her His arm and beckons her to come in with Him and taste His wine. This banquet hall pictures the church in jubilation, where we discover what it means to be inebriated with His love.

The Hebrew for **"banquet hall"** is "the House of Wine." This is the chamber of joy where love waves as a banner. The fruit of the apple tree now leads to the fruit of the vine. For the believer the House of Wine[4] is that place of experiencing the Holy Spirit. The King longs for her to know the Holy Spirit's power. He is taking her into the deeper experiences of the Holy Spirit.

The banquet hall brings the maiden into a new realm, into the house of wine. . . . She has never been to a church service like this before! The heavenlies are opened and she receives a foretaste of what their life will be like together. What liberty these guests have in the house of wine! Singing, rejoicing, and dancing; everyone seems so happy. Now she understands that this is what the Kingdom of God is like. Everyone seems so fulfilled in love, for they have been chosen to partake of the heavenly gift.

The King says, "Come, let *Me* take you to the House of Wine." Jesus is the One who takes us further into grace. Zeal alone will not bring us in, nor will our maturity bring us where we want to be . . . the King alone brings us in. It is His work to carry us when we are off the path like a wayward lamb. He will leave the ninety-nine to go after the one who goes astray (Luke 15:3). Often, wayward lambs kick and resist being taken further, until they renew their hearts to the King. The Bride is that lamb being carried on His shoulder into the chamber of joy.

The Flag Over Our Conquered Heart

"His banner over me is love . . . " She steps into the room, and suddenly a banner is unfurled over her head. This exquisite banner is displayed for all to see with the word **"Love"** written upon it. The King turns to His fiancée and says, "This flag is the banner of love that I have made to fly over your heart for all your days. It will picture the love relationship we will enjoy together forever. This will be the sign over you that you are blessed, protected, and covered. My banner over you is LOVE." Jesus has raised His flag of persistent, all-consuming love over her conquered heart.

When we discover we don't have to be perfect to be loved, that we are cherished simply because we said "yes" to Him, a flag is raised over our lives. If you look just above you now, you may be able to see it. Can you see His banner of eternal love? From this day forward, you must see the passion of God's heart towards you. The truth that strengthens us, the revelation that we live under, is the love of Jesus for weak, still imperfect Christians.

What furious love! What extravagant love! Disappointments no longer matter when you know this love. What others think of you will no longer mar your soul. When we are not appreciated or noticed we have a foundation beneath us and a banner over our heads. . . . There is a flag waving over my conquered heart that says, **"Love!"**

This furious love becomes the theme of our lives. We have a flag to follow, a banner to wave. When we are at our weakest, love abides. This is the banner we carry to the nations. This is the banner we carry to the broken and wounded. Omnipotent love has conquered us. We must wave this banner for all to see. . . .

How does it feel to see His banner flying over you in His House of Wine? What a celebration of love we can bring to the lonely of the world. Jesus is a King beyond belief.

Give Me More!

"Strengthen me with raisins, refresh me with apples . . . " She is seeking the Lord with fervency. She is asking to be strengthened to receive more of this love. Her cry is to be given a greater capacity to feel and know His love. Feelings of love can be very intense at times. Our aching, lovesick hearts must have more of Him. We desperately want to feel His embrace. The Holy Spirit Himself creates this longing that cannot be described. It is a love sickness. Go after your Lord Jesus with all your heart!

"Apples" represent the promises of the gospel. The words of Jesus are sweet and refreshing like apples. His promises to us can be compared to "apples of gold in settings of silver" (Prov. 25:11). They are aptly spoken into our need.

"His right arm embraces me, His left arm is under my head." The right arm is the manifest works of God that embrace us in ways we can see, feel, and discern. At His *right* hand are pleasures for evermore (Ps. 16:11). With His mighty right arm of power He touches us in love. We can thank Him for the unseen mercies that sustain us and the sweet manifestations of His touch that move us. How kind is our God. His embracing love is our confidence and our comfort.

The left arm is a picture of the invisible, unseen activity of God that sustains us. The left arm is away from our view, out of sight. There are so many things God does for us that we don't see.

God withholds things from us that would harm us. He is at work night and day to hold our heads secure in His love. Our God is so kind. The hands that hold the universe now hold the Shulamite maiden. Who could fear when held by a King like this?

The Bride rests her head until iniquity be done away. In this beautiful confidence she falls asleep in His arms. . . .

The True Sleeping Beauty!

The Shulamite has now become the true sleeping beauty. Overwhelmed by the power of the Spirit in the house of wine (engagement party) she falls asleep, content in the King's embrace. The King gazes upon the "sleeping beauty" as all the guests gather to look at her. The King whispers to His guests, **"Daughters of Jerusalem, I charge you by the gazelles and by the does of the field: Do not arouse or awaken love until she so desires."** Do not disturb her in this sleep of ecstasy; she is in love. Do not prematurely force her to "snap out of it" and return back to the frenzy of the church. The beauty of the King has enthralled her heart.

Many are jealous when they see another Christian in love with Jesus more passionately than they are. They want to disturb them, awaken them, and demand that they go out and toil like the rest of the vineyard-keepers. Others may even see you as lazy as you sit at His feet, but the Lord sees you as His very own . . . that is all that matters.

The word for **"gazelles"** in the Hebrew is "shabot" or 'hosts/armies'. This is the word used for the armies of God. The Lord has an army of gazelles! Those who truly follow the Lord will be tender of heart, like our Lord Jesus. Gazelles harm no one; they are truly beautiful creatures . . . so the Lord's armies are comprised of those men and women who are gentle of spirit.

Because fellowship with Jesus is so lovely, the King uses the figure of the loveliest of creatures in exhorting the daughters of Jerusalem to refrain from disturbing the resting Bride. Who would want to drive away the beautiful gazelle? Who would want to disturb the Bride while she is lost in holy love with Jesus? It is time to rest and find her delight in this divine embrace.

The season will soon change, but for now she must cultivate deep intimacy with her Bridegroom. When we are in this stage of our lives, we are not even aware of what is going on around us. We seem to forget that many are headed for destruction . . . the nations are needing the message of life. Meanwhile we think that we are saved for only one purpose . . . personal pleasure. Sacrifice, warfare, discipline; those are all strange terms to us when we are sitting under the apple tree enjoying the feast of fellowship. But this self-absorbed stage must eventually give way to the development of true character and maturity. We must be equipped and trained to rule as the co-heir of all things.

So, the King will soon come to the sleeping Shulamite to call her forward. . . . But is she ready to go?

---

5. The fir tree was also called the "death tree" for its common use for casket making.

6. It was a "thorn bush" from which God spoke to Moses. In the midst of the thorns of our flesh life, God would place fire within the heart of His passionate ones... like He did with Moses.

7. Jesus said that thorns are also those things that choke the SEED and keep it from bearing fruit (Matt. 13:26).

8. At the traditional Jewish betrothal ceremony, the bride and groom drink from the same cup of wine. The banquet hall is where the King proposes to His Bride. This is what Jesus did with His disciples at the last supper.

Arise, My Darling

Chapter 2:8-17
ℬℭ

𝒩ow it is time to see Him in a new light. Jesus has many faces, many expressions of Himself. He is the Lion and the Lamb, the Alpha and Omega, the Bridegroom and the Judge. He is transcendent, infinitely higher than our highest thought of Him. About the time you think you have Jesus figured out, He appears in a way you do not expect. The maiden has so much to learn about this Shepherd-King; and so do we.

Sweet apples, sitting under the shade tree, the House of Wine, the Banner of Love, being wooed by the Son of God—life is really happening for her. Things are great. Spending time with this Soul-Satisfying Savior named Jesus—what could be better? She has seen His affection for her; she has felt the exhilaration of His love. But for her, Jesus is still the means, not the end. She is in this for her. Most of her declarations still have *her* as the theme, not Him. It is as though He exists only for *her* pleasure. There is much yet for her to learn—so much more!

Jesus wants a mature partner, not just a girlfriend. He desires to have a marriage, not a date. We must be prepared to sit with Him on His throne. Our compromises will have to go, our limited understanding must be enlarged, and our knowledge of Him must increase. The King patiently leads her from one test to the next, equipping her in perfect love.

The Banner over her is always *"Love."* She will need to remember this throughout all the tests that come. Love disciplines us and changes us. Love matures us and makes us like Him. The rest of this book will describe the answer to her prayer, *"Draw me, and I will run after You."* Now He comes to invite her to run with Him as a new season begins in her journey. . . .

Ready or not, here He comes!

He is the searching One, looking for His Beloved. First she hears His voice, and then she sees His power. He is awakening her by His voice . . . or is it His song? She recognizes the voice of her Beloved. Others may tell her many things; but it is only the voice of the Beloved that will pierce her inner ear. Jesus comes to her with an entirely new look. It is time for her to see Him in a new dimension.

In her amazement we hear her exclaim, "Look! Here He comes, leaping over the mountaintops. Wow, I have never seen Him do this before. My beloved, what are you doing on the mountains? I thought you liked shade trees and feeding me apples?"

She is stirred by the voice of her Leaping Prince. Who is this that jumps effortlessly over the mountains, bounding over the hills? He is so much more than she ever dreamed Him to be. Jesus Christ is the Leaping Lord of Glory! Mountains, hills, barriers, obstacles—they are nothing to Him. He knows nothing of discouragement or difficulty. So strong is His love for her, nothing could hold Him back. He will leap effortlessly over the mountains of her unbelief, skipping over the hills of her struggles as though they were nothing. With His voice of power, He can speak to the mountains and they will be removed.

This is not merely the sweet, soul-satisfying Savior coming to her; this is the Sovereign King who lets nothing stand in His way. How energetic and agile He is. . . . How mighty and regal! This Warrior-King is totally victorious and cannot be intimidated by her difficulties (mountains, hills).

What hinders her is nothing to Him! Jesus wants to show her His omnipotent resurrection power—for only God could leap over mountaintops. Mountains of adversity are nothing to your Beloved. He will come no matter where you are, and sweep you off your feet. He skips over all the plans the enemy has designed to hinder you. He leaps over every obstacle with ease. He is the Resurrected, Sovereign King over all the nations!

He comes to the maiden to lead her to the mountaintops. Will she go with Him? Is she ready to pay the price? It is time for the Bride to leave the cozy corner under the shade tree. The Leaping Lord will come to challenge our comfort zone and beckon us to come away in sacrificial service. Jesus wants a mountain-leaping partner. He has an agenda to fulfill. The nations must be won and discipled by the King.

Jesus calls us to a life that is risky, inconvenient, and self-sacrificing. We must be His partners in going to the nations, running together on the hills. We cannot just love Him at a distance; we must have a history of running together in resurrection power. It is time to realize that we are not in this just for our own spiritual pleasure.

Jesus wants to disciple a Bride into maturity, living for *His* pleasure. It is good to learn the sweetness of communion, but now we must receive power for service. A fierce struggle of spiritual warfare is all around us—it will require a brave, courageous Bride that is willing to go to the mountains with her Beloved.

"My Lover is like a gazelle or a young stag." The gazelle is swift and sure-footed. This is a new revelation of Jesus to the Bride. A gazelle walks on high places. The inscription of Psalm 22 reads, "To the Doe (Gazelle) of the morning." This speaks of Christ's resurrection. Jesus is the Gazelle who leaped out of the dark tomb on Resurrection morning. He skips in resurrection power! The maiden begins to recognize His strength and agility to overcome every obstacle. He is coming to bid her to arise and go with Him in that same power. Jesus loves you so much He will climb mountains just to be with you . . . even a mountain called Calvary. This is love.

"Look! There he stands behind our wall." For the first time there is a wall between her and her Lord. She now sees that she is not as close to Him as she once thought. She calls it "our wall," but the truth is — *she* is the one hiding behind the wall! He is out on the mountains and hills, skipping freely in His eternal triumph. Her wall of self-protection has become a wall of hiding.

When we put up walls to protect us from pain, we are actually shutting ourselves off from the presence of the Healer. But even the wall we so carefully construct will not hinder Him. He will come and stand behind our wall waiting for us to yield (Ps. 18:29). In this new season of maturing love, the Bride will be challenged to leave her walls and run with Him.

A wall is what we see when we look inwardly. *Seeing ourself is like seeing a wall.* We begin to notice inside of us all the things that shut Him out and keep us from sacred intimacy with Jesus.

Jesus looks into me and sees my walls, yet He is still patient and kind in all His ways. His love is a "window" through which He sees us as we really are; truly in love with Him! Can't you see Jesus gazing on His Bride? He stands beside her walls, **"gazing through the windows, peering through the lattice."** He looks into her eyes (windows to the soul) and sees that she loves Him, even though she is not yet ready to leave her comfort zone. She wants to hide behind the wall and make sure she is safe.

As we will see, she says no. . . . He can see it in her eyes. He can hear her thoughts: "I'm afraid of mountain climbing. I am not ready yet. Let me stay here for a while under the shade of Your apple tree. I'm happy here . . . I'm satisfied; can't we just sit here together and enjoy one another? Let someone else leap on the mountains and go to the nations. I'll just linger here with You. . . . "

Love Calls Her Higher

"Arise my darling." Every time He speaks to her it is with tender love. How we wish all of God's servants could follow in our Shepherd's example. He calls her His beautiful one, His darling. Yet there is hesitancy in her eyes as He peers into her heart. . . . What is it that makes her lovely to Him? Jesus acknowledges the virtues that are only budding within her. . . . He will never close His heart to her. . . . Never!

God does not define your life by the ten percent of you that you hold back from Him, but by the ninety percent of your spirit that says "yes" to Him continually. Aren't you glad? Your weakness is covered by the torrent of His Love. He doesn't say, "Why, you hypocrite. You only *think* you love Me. What is this hesitancy I see in your eyes? You are so stubborn and incomplete in your devotion to Me. Your fear and sin makes you ugly."

You will never hear words like that from your Beloved! Even in your failures He holds you fast. He calls you beautiful . . . long before you see His beauty forming in your life. He calls you His darling . . . long before you feel that you are close to Him. You are safe with a King like this. Jesus' love is what imparts the strength to arise and come away. His fiery love has power to break off every desire for the "world" and its artificial pleasures. His love will consume every other ambition and passion. How can we cling to our "dust," when He bids us *"Arise"*?

If He calls me His darling, if He counts me fair and worthy of being His love partner, who am I to hold back behind my wall? How can I linger among the goats of Kedar when He calls me to the mountaintops? *"Come with Me. Come away further and further with Me. Come away from everything selfish and sinful. Come away with Me from the religious systems and structures of men to be My Bridal Partner. Come with Me into the mystery of higher life in the Spirit.* **Come with Me.**"

This message has no harsh sound to my ear. What could hold me back in this wilderness? To come away with Him is to come home from exile, to come to shore from the raging storm, to come to strength and shelter out of my place of weakness. We must be those who pray: "Lord, send Your mighty Spirit to kindle fresh fires of love in my heart until I leave this place of hiding and come away with You."

Beloved one, this is not the time to be hiding behind your wall; this is the time to be learning the ways of the Leaping Lord Jesus. It is time to leave the predictable things behind and launch out into the undiscovered country of end-time ministry. Jesus is ready for action. Comforts and human securities must be abandoned as we leave for the high place. We are to be carried by love to a higher place, a greener pasture, a quieter stream. We have not seen it all yet.

But the maiden is afraid of heights; she doesn't like the mountains. She prefers the couch, resting behind her walls, being fed with apples, and staying safe in her comfort zone. He wants her to walk on mountains; she prefers the couch. Sound familiar? She is not yet ready to go. . . .

What are the things that hold us back from pursuing Jesus? The risks of walking in faith! Jesus requires that we risk all in our walk of faith. The voice of the Lord once said to me, "Brian, I have not called you to play it safe." The wild frontier is unpredictable and untamed, but this is where we must go to get to our Promised Land.

Bold faith is always the way of God's Kingdom, operating in the confidence of invisible things (II Cor. 5:7, 4:18). Risky? Yes, but we honor God every time we trust in His integrity. It is a mysterious way to run a Kingdom, but this is God's chosen way of drawing us into true devotion to Him. We will not grow until we venture out from our comfort zone and encounter Him in a place of weakness and trust.

"My Lover . . . said . . . Arise, my darling, my beautiful one . . . " No one has ever spoken to her this way . . . with such tenderness! He enjoys her as His darling while she is growing, not after she is mature. She has not even said yes to His invitation, yet she is still His beautiful darling.

Let this truth wash over you again: Jesus enjoys the immature believer. As a father enjoys his growing child, so He enjoys you from the moment your heart said "yes" to Him. She is still behind her wall on the couch hiding from Him. But He knows what is in her heart . . . and He knows what love He has for her.

Jesus called her beautiful while she is in the process of growing in mature love. A loving father enjoys his child during the messy stages of its life. Immature and clumsy, unable to clean up after himself . . . but still he is loved by his dad. So it is with our Heavenly Father; there is no mess He will not clean up for His children. Only believe and walk forward into the fire of His love. He enjoys the responsive heart of love, not the particular stage of maturity we are in. God knew we would linger in immaturity when He called us! But given time, immature love will bud and grow into maturity. *Remember,* at each stage of our growth Jesus calls us **"My darling . . . My beautiful one."**

Seven Prophetic Signs

The King now gives her seven prophetic signs of Resurrection Life. He is sharing these secrets with her so that she will arise and come with Him. These words are meant to assure her of His power, and of the approaching harvest:

1. **"The winter is past."** The chill of a gloomy and angry winter is past. The cold winds of trials no longer blow. If He was faithful during the winter of discontent, He will be faithful in the springtime of budding grace. The warmth of love has come with new hope. Jesus asks, "Why are you afraid? I took you through the winter, and we are still together. I will take you into spring." The kindness of Jesus in our winter season assures us that we will be safe in the springtime of dawning purpose.

2. **"The rains are over and gone."** The rivers are no longer flooding. The cold winter rains of difficulty and inconvenience are over and gone; they have completed their task of soaking the soil. No longer muddy and dirty, we walk on new ground. All of nature is responsive to the return of summer . . . but will she respond to His love and run away with Him?

3. **"Flowers appear on the earth."** In Matthew 6 we learn that flowers bring the message of God's care. Flowers appear on the vine just before the fruit is harvested. The flowers are prophetic signs of a soon-to-come harvest. The King is urging her not to remain an immature girl when He needs a mature partner to harvest the nations with the Gospel. There is urgency in His voice . . . she must make herself ready as destiny breaks forth on the earth. As flowers blossom all around her, there is no time to waste in joining her King in His mission. . . . Her destiny is on the horizon.

4. **"The season of singing has come."** A time of celebration is breaking forth. In Isaiah 54:1-3, the barren woman is commanded to sing even before she gives birth. The power of prophetic song prepares hearts for harvest. The new thing God is unfolding will require new songs to be sung. The season of singing and dancing is here. How could you hold back when Jesus sings His Song of Songs over you?

5. **"The cooing of doves is heard in our land."** This spiritual spring brings the soothing messages of love to our souls; it is like the cooing of doves! The Dove has come to sing to our spirits and awaken us in bridal affection for the Son. As this "cooing" touches our hearts, we arise and prepare ourselves for His approach. We are told that the turtledove always sings at harvest time! If you listen carefully today, you will hear the cooing of doves in our land. His Kingdom of Love is coming to the earth.

6. **"The fig tree forms its early fruit."** The fig tree is a prophetic sign throughout the Bible. Jesus taught us that when the fig tree begins to bud it shows that

summer is near, even at the door (Matt. 24:32-33). Figs will grow even in the wintertime. The fruit of the fig tree is a picture of what has been matured and tested during the winter seasons of your life. The early fruit is forming on the trees . . . Jesus sees His fruit coming forth in you.

7. **"The blossoming vines spread their fragrance."** This speaks of the thriving grace of God that is upon us for "the blossoming vines" are releasing the scent of spring. The visible signs of future fruitfulness are upon us as Jesus sees His Bride as a vine covered with blossoms. The fragrance of tender grapes is starting to come forth. The Bridegroom calls His fiancée to share His joy in these fragrant tokens of heavenly life that are springing forth.

As the Bride-to-be hesitates behind her wall, the Bridegroom repeats His invitation to come and run with her King. She must leave herself behind and follow Him in resurrection power as they skip over mountains together. He urges her to step out in faith and prepare for the end-time harvest. The power of the book of Acts is about to be released for the Bride in end-time power. An *"Acts 29"* church is going to arise and you are going to be needed for leadership in His glorious outpouring.

She has so much yet to learn. He is telling her: "Can't you see all the signs of the harvest? Don't draw back now . . . I want you with Me on the mountaintops." He woos her with bridal love. With no threats, with only love, He draws her forward. This is ever the way of our Heavenly Bridegroom. Jesus will consistently motivate us with affirmation and grace, not fear and condemnation. Love lifts us higher, much higher than fear of rejection; but we must respond. . . .

Embraced In Her Weakness

He can see it in her eyes . . . she's not going to leave her comfort zone; she can't do it. Like Peter, He could tell her that she is going to betray His love and stay behind. Yet in her weak moment, struggling with fear, He reveals His tender heart of affection.

It would be hard to find in Scripture a more powerful statement of the heart of Jesus towards weak, fearful, and immature believers than right here. . . . He calls her **"My dove."** Embraced in her weakness, He describes His love for her as David wrote in Psalm 68:13, *"Even while you sleep among the campfires, the wings of My dove are sheathed with silver, its feathers with shining gold."*

The dove is a bird that speaks of purity, innocence, peace, and loyalty. A dove never mates again after its partner dies. He affirms to her that she belongs to Him, and that she will never be content unless they are running together. However the loyal dove is not a term WE would use to describe her now from a human perspective . . . but the Bridegroom is gazing into her heart. He doesn't call her a slimy snake, but His pet dove. His heart is ever reaching towards her even as she hides in fear. Each statement from His heart tells her that He is safe, He can be trusted.

"In the clefts of the rock, in the hiding places . . . " Jesus sees His Bride-to-be as a precious dove hidden in the clefts of the rock. She is nestled in the secret place of the stairs, safe in the hiding places of His love. He has made for her a nest, a dwelling place on high. Within the wounded side of her Lord, all is safe and secure. She was made to soar with Him as His partner for life.

It is time to leave the nest and fly with Him over the mountaintops. Jesus calls each of us to come and fly with Him from the secret place as we go together to the nations with the message of love, the **"cooing of doves."**

Moses was hidden in the clefts of the rock while the glory of God passed by. This was a foreshadowing of our redemption. Moses hiding in the clefts of the rock was a type of salvation through the cross. Jesus is the Rock that was cleft, or pierced for us (I Cor. 10:4). Nestled in His wounded side, we find shelter from the blazing holiness of God that would destroy us in our sins. Jesus sees the maiden as one who is hidden in the cross. His wounds are our hiding place. Our true life is here in this hidden nest on high (Col. 3:1-4). Fully identified with the cross of Jesus, with no wall of self-protection; this is how Jesus views us.

As she takes her place in the Cleft Rock, the things of self and flesh are broken to pieces. Here she will receive heavenly vision and spiritual sight. This Rock must be her Stronghold and Dwelling Place. United to the cross, she can live above the circumstances of life with its pain and testing. There will be Water gushing from this Rock, which will satisfy her and wash her from all defilement. *This verse is the call of the Cross*—to live in the nest as one crucified and raised again to sit on high.

The words used here are actually, *"in the secret place of the stairs."* There is an ascending life awaiting her. Jesus is her "stairway." He is the Heavenly Escalator that Jacob dreamed about (Gen. 28:12 & John 1:51).

This secret stairway is the place of mystery. She has not understood the mysteries of God nor the ascended life. Jesus Christ is clearly the ladder that reaches from earth (His human nature) to heaven (His heavenly nature). Jesus spoke to Nathaniel using the same terminology— *"I tell you the truth, you shall see heaven open, and the angels of God ascending and descending upon the Son of Man"* (John 1:51).

Jacob received the glorious revelation that Jesus is the STAIRWAY to heaven! By Him we climb the steep pathway and leave this lower life. It is when we see Him that the Father speaks to our hearts. All of God's favors come to us on this Jesus-Ladder. Jesus is the only valid entry into the spirit realm. He is the way into the heavenlies. Before the Shulamite can be a "sent one" to the nations she must see herself as 'nested' in the secret place of the stairs!

Come to Me in Your Weakness

Now that we are secure in the clefts of the Rock, Jesus can freely share His heart with us. He looks at our timid heart and says, **"Show Me your face . . . "** God wants us to run to Him in our weakness, not away from Him in fear. He asks of us: "Let me gaze into your eyes. Show Me your face."

As the Bridegroom looks upon her even in her brokenness He can see His reflection shining forth. From her place in the hidden stairway, her face is lovely to Him. Instead of hearing a lecture she is washed in love.

He pleads with her further to look into His eyes: **"Show Me your face, let Me hear your voice."** How her voice moves His heart! He wants to hear her adoring worship and her prayer for help in the coming time of crisis. This is an invitation for her to intercede and cry out to Him; to worship Him even in her place of need. "If only you knew how sweet your voice is from the clefts of the Rock. How lovely you look there hidden in my love. Let me hear your heart's cry and I will answer you. Your voice is music to My ears, sweet, pleasing and acceptable to Me."

Instead of her voice sounding repulsive to His heart, her worship and intercession are **"sweet"** to the Lord. May He hear our voice and call it sweet.

"Your face is lovely." Jesus loves you like there is no one else to love; He loves you even as the Father loves Him. He is looking into your face and sees love in your eyes. Even though you may feel that you are immature, tentative, and hesitating, you are lovely to the King. He is telling you,

"It is time to let Me enjoy you. You have focused on your satis-faction and what I am to you. Now bring your sweetness to My Spirit, for your face is lovely and **"your voice is sweet."** *Let me take pleasure in you."*

Jesus always finds delight in His times of fellowship with you and I. Can you imagine Jesus looking at you where you are today and saying: "I enjoy you, I admire your beauty, I love you! Arise from your self-life and let me break your shackles of introspection and fear that keep you distant from Me. Give Me your worship, for it is sweet. . . . " Just think, Jesus calls your prayer life sweet. . . .

Deal With Compromise

As we rest with Him in the cleft of the Rock, enjoying the comfort of His presence, He is now free to tell us how we can ascend the secret stairway. . . . **"Catch for us the foxes, the little foxes . . . "**

In every love relationship there will be things that hinder love. They can be habits, words, and weaknesses; areas of our lives that will spoil the freshness of love in our hearts. We want to obey Him. We really want to leave our mess and go with Him, but what about the foxes, the compromises, the remaining issues that hinder our spiritual advancement?

He is not addressing the "lions" of rebellion but the subtle areas that seem so little. There are no little sins to God. There is no area that is off limits to the Holy Spirit. Everything is significant when the Lord speaks to us about it.

Jesus says, **"Catch for us;"** it is a joint project. He will help us and show us where the foxes of compromise hide (Ps. 139:23). Jesus comes to us and says, "It is time for a fox hunt. . . . It is time to remove those areas of darkness in your heart so that the garden within you is not ruined." Foxes come out at night (hidden areas) and spoil the vines. If unnoticed and ignored, these "little foxes" will destroy the blooming buds of new life. Tie their tails together like Samson did and put the torch of truth to the wood, hay, and stubble of your self-life!

We all have "little" areas that destroy a life of fruitfulness. Each pocket of compromise must be dealt with. Every entanglement and weight upon our souls must be shaken off so that we can run our race with endurance and swiftness.

Some of the little foxes or "little folly" (Eccl. 10:1) that will ruin the inner life are: foolishness, pride, spreading slander, anger, laziness, wasting time, worldly thinking, speaking too quickly, defending ourself, being touchy or critical toward others, a negative and complaining spirit, impatience, neglect of prayer, exaggeration, self-importance, an independent spirit—all of these must be thoroughly caught and removed or the budding fruits of new life will be hindered. Remember that foxes are cunning and crafty animals and so is your flesh life. We catch the lions and the bears but miss the foxes.

"My Lover is mine . . . " Her sincere love is expressed even in this moment of stumbling. She sees the compromises. She sees His love. She sees the risks. She sees her need. Despite it all she declares that He belongs to her, and she belongs to Him. When we feel failure and are trapped in compromise, this must be our confession: "My Lover is mine, and I am His!" Foxes or no foxes, our Lord Jesus belongs to us in our imperfect condition. This revelation is what will give her confidence in days to come to catch the little foxes and remove them from her garden. . . .

Her first priority is still to possess Him for her own pleasure. Her love remains immature. She will follow Him as long as where He leads is pleasing and comfortable to her. Rather than arising to run away, her thoughts turn to her place of security with Him. Her thoughts are: "You are already mine . . . why should I be troubled and have to go to the mysterious mountains to learn more of You? I already belong to You alone. . . . I know where I can find You anytime I want You . . . feeding among the lilies."

She has yet to experience a true dying to self and brokenness of the outer life. Her own inner satisfaction means more to her at this time than leaping with the Lord on the hills. Yet even as she speaks, revelation comes to her: **"My Lover is mine, *and I am His."***

She begins to understand, "Not only do You belong to me, but I belong to You. You have an inheritance in me, just as I have an inheritance in You. I really do live to serve You." What a glorious revelation it is when we see ourselves as His! You are the Father's love gift to the Son. You are His heritage, His chosen one, His Bride. Jesus gave His sacred blood to purchase your soul. . . . Each crimson drop spilled on the cross speaks of *this* love that made you His.

You are everything He died for, and He will have you fully. He fought for you, defying all the hosts of hell, which made you their prey. He conquered your sins, and then He went on to conquer *you,* so that you might be His happy captive, His prisoner of hope! You may now say with all your heart: **"I am His!"** You could belong to no other. You do not belong to the world; you live for the world above! You do not even belong to the church; you belong to the Great Shepherd. You do not belong to sin, self, or Satan. You belong exclusively and entirely to Him.

When another comes to steal your heart, you may say, "I am already engaged. My Lover is mine, and I am His." Let this sink in. . . . The brightness of God's glory, the Lord Jesus Christ, is all yours! He is yours in His greatness, yours in His sinless and pure life, yours in all that He was, all that He is, and all that He shall ever be. He is not just yours to talk about, or even talk to . . . but yours to commune with, as a Friend. Yours in every dark moment and every happy day. Yours when you know it, and yours when you doubt it. He is yours in His glory—forever yours.

"He browses among the lilies." This is where you will always find Him, among the lilies of His Paradise. Jesus loves to find peace among His people of pure heart—they are His lilies. He is refreshed by your loving fellowship. In poetic imagery we learn the sacred truth that dearest communion with Jesus can never be known by the hard and restless ways of an unbroken heart. This is the priceless heritage of the meek and lowly—those who are like His guarded garden. Like a doe that grazes in a field of white lilies is the Lord of Heaven among those with gentle spirit. He longs to feed us the deep things of His Spirit, as we walk with Him in purity.

The inscription of Psalm 45 states that it was written, *"To the tune of lilies."* The lilies do not toil, spin, or fear. He calls her His lily. Light is starting to come into her soul. She finds that He really is nothing to fear. He will provide her safety, even on the dark trail leading into the night. She realizes, 'My love can feed His heart. . . . I could become His lily, His place of communion (browsing). He could catch the foxes. . . . We could catch them together.'

Yet, even with the dawning of this revelation, she says "No." Her focus is still on herself. Her destiny beckons her to come forth, but she is not ready. She must endure the pain of His withdrawal to understand what she is missing. . . .

Her Painful Refusal

"Until the day breaks and the shadows flee, turn, my Lover, and be like a gazelle or like a young stag on the rugged hills" (Literally, "the hills of Bether"). She answers, "No, I cannot go. You go ahead without me. Turn, be like a gazelle on the rugged hills. I am not ready to leave this predictable place to run with You. You are still my Lover, but I am afraid. Perhaps later, when the shadows (doubts and fears) flee and the full light comes I will go. When the Day breaks and fills the sky with light, perhaps *then* I could run with You. Turn . . . go by yourself to the mountains of separation (Bether means "separation.") I must stay . . . go be like a gazelle. . . . "

She is not prepared to go with Him. After the cooing of doves is heard, her heart still holds back. She is a reluctant and preoccupied bride. . . .

How often does this take place with you and I? We think we need to grow more, to wait until the clouds lift and the darkness flees. We want to see better before we take off into the undiscovered country of growing in Christ. It's hard to walk in the twilight of our immaturity. We tell Jesus to go on ahead without us and leap across the mountains in resurrection strength; we must grow more. "Go on ahead, Jesus, I'll catch up with you later." We want the Lord to be with us in our circumstances. We want Jesus there in our pain, when we need Him. "Jesus, can't you stay here with me in this cozy, comfortable place behind my wall and make me feel better?"

But why aren't we ready to say "yes" when He needs us to run with Him to the nations? He has plans in His heart for us. . . .

How could we say no? We presume that we could do a better job of leading our life than He can. We want to be in charge of our destiny and direct our path. But true and lasting transformation comes when Jesus is our Destiny and our Path.

She has much to learn. *We* have much to learn. Her mind is set on the future — **"until."** "Someday I'll be His delight and skip with Him on the mountains, but not now. Life is hard and I need to protect myself and hide behind my wall." We must never wait until the imperfections (shadows) flee. Now is the time to arise and run! We run out of the shadows into His light. Our lamps must be trimmed and filled with oil. When we see Him, the shadows have already fled away by the light of His brilliance. The new day has already dawned; the Bridegroom is in the land. As we follow Him, our paths will be like the first rays of dawn that shine more and more until the perfect day (Prov. 4:18). The supernatural life awaits you . . . will you go?

Upon hearing her words...with His heart breaking, He turns away slowly into the night. He leaves her to go up the dark trail . . . alone. . . .

He Hides for a Season

Chapter 3:1-11
ಬಾ೦ಚ

*O*nce you have tasted His fruit and held Him in the arms of sacred intimacy, you will never want Him to leave. But Father knows best. God knows just how to mature us through seasons of bountiful blessings and seasons of discipline and dryness. The maiden will learn well the lesson of what happens when we say "No" to the invitation of Jesus. . . . We are not rejected, but it can be lonely in that self-made wilderness of wanting our own way. . . .

"All night long . . . I looked for the One my heart loves. . . . " Her refusal to go to the mountains with Jesus brings a sleepless night. She had seen Him turn away to walk alone to the high place. For a season, He is hidden from her. There are times when God strategically hides His face from us. He withdraws the *awareness* of His presence to draw our hearts toward Him. This is a form of Divine instruction to the soul. Often it happens when we need Him the most. We feel vulnerable, forgotten. Our feelings betray us and eventually confusion can set in.

Although we rarely interpret these times as "training," yet it is God's way of disciplining those He dearly loves. Depression often hits us when we no longer feel close to Jesus. He is always there and we know His Word is true, yet we *feel* far from Him. Temptations to return to old habits will intensify during these times of discipline. "Where did He go?" At times, the devil may try to convince us that God doesn't really care about what is happening. Disappointment clings to our soul. We begin to mistake His discipline for rejection, but Love is strong, even in the season of discipline. What are we to do in times like these? We must seek Him even in the dark . . . when we don't feel Him. This is the key that turns darkness to light.

The Shulamite maiden continues to pray on her bed behind her wall of isolation. The phrase **"all night long"** is literally "night after night." This is not merely one sleepless night, but a *season* of discipline in her life. This "night" is a time of darkness and separation for her. She feels the remorse for saying "goodbye" to the One she loves. How oppressed we can feel in times like these! Seeking Him in our "night seasons" will create a desperation in our hearts. It causes us to overcome the natural tendency to sleep (backslide) and push away inconvenience to find our Beloved.

"I looked for the One my heart loves." This is the title she gives Jesus. Her love for Him is strong, even in the night seasons of her life. When confusion and restlessness enters her heart, she still reaches out to find Him. There is no desire more powerful than the longing of a soul to know Jesus. Love for Jesus will break the power of a thousand sins. Once you have tasted the sweet wine of His love, pursuing Him is all you can do. Have you been touched by an unrelenting passion to hold Him? Your "night" season has been designed to draw you deeper into Him . . . until you cry out: *"My soul yearns for you in the night"* (Isa. 26:9).

What are the lessons of the night season? We are led into a deeper honesty—a searching of our hearts for what drove Him from us. Often there are undiscerned issues — hidden faults that must be discovered or we will continue to grieve the Holy Spirit. These seasons produce a more sincere humility in us. We are forced to see our weakness and live by faith. No one lives with unbroken feelings of God's presence. We all must lean on Him as our source of godly emotions.

Jesus wants a Bride He can show off to the universe — a Bride worthy to share His throne! This requires repeated dealings from God. Often it seems we are bruised in life, wondering why God is distant and detached from our pain. This is all a Divine setup to make us desperate for Jesus alone. Someday He will show you off to all the universe and say of you, "See what my love has brought forth! Satan has no place in her (John 14:30). I have conquered her fears; I have brought her forth in Holy Passion to sit with Me on my Throne. Father, here is my Bride!"

Love Conquers Her Fear

"I will get up now. . . . " Love for Jesus conquers her fear of the night. She determines to arise and seek Him, nothing could keep her back now. She disobeyed the command to arise in 2:13 and go to the mountains. Now she understands what it costs her to miss the call of God. We often think of how much it will cost to obey. We seem to conveniently forget about the cost of disobedience.

Lack of discipline costs more than being disciples. He has chastened her by withdrawing the sense of His presence. There are three responses we can have to this discipline:

1. We can take it lightly.
   (But He means business!)

2. We can take it too heavily.
   (Faint not! He only disciplines those He dearly loves).

3. We can endure the discipline and learn the lesson.
   (He is truly tender and compassionate.)

The pain of losing His presence motivates her to arise from her bed in the middle of the night and go after Him. **"I will get up now and go about the city."** She is incurably devoted to Jesus, unable to live without Him. Is this how you feel when life is difficult? Do you shake off your slumber and seek Him? Or does self-pity keep you bound?

We ache over the distance between where we are and where we want to be. How can we continue to lay here another day in lethargy when He has called us to arise? Yes, it is hard to get up in the middle of the night, but it is much harder to live apart from the sweet communion of being with Jesus (Acts 4:13). The glorious freshness of time with Him cannot be compared to being comfortable behind our wall. Arise, beloved, and search for Him!

The "city" is a picture of the church (Heb. 12:22). The city of God speaks of the purpose and destiny of God for our lives (Heb. 11:10). The corporate activity of people is in a city **(its streets and squares)**. The church, like a city, has government (elders) and order. Her desperation for Jesus drives her to involve herself again with others.

We will always find Him in fellowship with His flock, His people. Jesus loves messed up people. To avoid fellowship with other believers is to avoid Him, for He dwells with His people. When our hunger reaches the point where we cannot stand our self-imposed isolation any longer, Jesus brings us into His "city" to reveal Himself to us. There is a risk in moving about in this city.

People can harm us and wound us, but this is where we must go to seek Him.

"The watchmen found me as they made their rounds. . . . " The watchmen are keepers of the "city" (church). They are the true spiritual shepherds who watch over our souls (Heb. 13:17, Ezek. 3:17, Isa. 62:6). Watchmen are responsible for overseeing the affairs of the city and for watching over that city so enemies do not attack it. The safety of the city (or church) is entrusted to these heaven sent watchmen. These are the same ones He referred to as "shepherds" in 1:8.

She is now recognizing spiritual authority in the Body. They are *true spiritual shepherds* doing their duty. They find her troubled, distraught as she questions them, **"Have you seen the One my heart loves?"** She had lost His presence; perhaps they could help her. She humbles herself before them as she asks for their help.

Our Lord Jesus is serious about issues of spiritual authority and utilizing team ministry. This is how His kingdom operates. Many problems arise when we ignore these truths. So the Shulamite looks to the watchmen asking, "Have you seen Him?" This is the question sincerely asked to today's shepherds over God's flocks. Leaders are only capable of leading when they have seen Him. "Have you seen Him. . . . Do you KNOW Him. . . . Is He living in you?"

Finding Her Beloved

"Scarcely had I passed them. . . . I found the One my heart loves." There are times we must go beyond the watchmen in order to find the One we love. Watchmen are a blessing, but they are not Him. We may love the watchmen, those who minister to us, but no one can take His place. Our deepest, fondest, purest love is saved for Him. When she is able to see beyond them, she found

Him! He suddenly renews His sweet love to her heart. She is thrilled to find Him again. It was worth going out into the dark night to seek for the Beloved. The Lord is faithful and good. He was only waiting for her to come to Him. Love brought her near. Jesus makes Himself easy to find to the seeking soul!

"I held Him and would not let Him go. . . . " This is a deeper experience than just finding Him. We must *hold* Him dear. Clinging to Him, she resolves never to let this happen again. The pain of her spiritual darkness taught her a great lesson. How do we hold Him? In the power of holy resolve.

This is what our Lord said in John 15: *"abide in Me."* Likewise, the disciples on the Emmaus road urged Him strongly, *"Stay with us."* We must not only run after Him, we must hold Him tightly once we have found Him. With Jacob's boldness we must cling to Him until the shadows flee . . . as poor sinners holding onto Omnipotence!

Have you let Him go? It is comparatively easy to climb the mountain of His presence than it is to stay there. Jesus tells us:

"Abide in Me." To remain with Him each moment, clinging in grace to His hand — this is our goal and delight. A branch does not come and go, but it remains with the vine, connected to its source. Our lives are too filled with moments of letting Him go. Real love will cling to Him . . . No matter what.

Your Beloved is willing to be held. . . . He loves your "sacred violence" that will take Him by force! Faith and love holds Him fast. Wrap your golden chains of love around Him, and He will abide with you. . . .

The rest of the story is the outworking of holding on to Him. She deeply resolves to never consciously turn her back on Him again. A new zeal enters her spirit to keep Him near her heart. This "holy violence" causes us to prevail (hold on to Him) until we break through our barriers into kingdom living (Matt. 11:12, Gen. 32:26). There are times when God will only respond to us when we have a holy resolution burning within us. Our intense love conquers His heart and He moves to lift us higher in grace. He will not refuse such focused longing. Like Mary did in the garden, when you find Him, hold Him tight.

"**. . . till I had brought Him to my mother's house.**" The church is our "mother's house." Jesus is the husband of His house. Those who do His will are known as His "mother" and "brother" (Matt. 12:46-50). In Revelation 12:5, the woman giving birth to the man-child is the church (See also Gal. 4:6). She longs to take Him into every relationship,into the familiar setting of church-life. Oddly enough, it is can be sometimes very difficult to take Jesus into church with us . . . It is where we get wounded by others. Relationships are tested, even strained at times.

The maiden wants to hold onto Him (assimilate His life) until it touches every relationship in the family of God. You must become one who brings Him to others in the Body of Christ. Your love for Him qualifies you. If your soul is so in love with Jesus that you cannot possibly live without Him, you will become one who releases that love in the Church. Grasp Him in love and take Him with you as you walk with others in the local church. Bringing Jesus to her home (church) is the first manifestation of the maiden's new obedience. Jesus brought her into His chambers (1:4), now she is bringing Jesus into her mother's chambers.

"**Do not awaken. . . .** " The King puts a "Do Not Disturb" sign over her soul and charges the people to leave her alone during this season of renewed intimacy. There are times when we need not trouble the tender soul with fervent serving when they are in a season of sacred intimacy. Often we misread what God is doing with another, because we do not have enough discernment to really know what His plan may be in the life of another.

The **"daughters of Jerusalem"** are the immature believers who do not understand the various operations of the Spirit. It is a mistake to disturb them with our premature judgments. Spending time with Jesus and drawing from His life is the very thing that will transform the weakest saint. God is making us into mature co-workers with Jesus who will disciple the nations. This requires times of serenity and times of service. Wisdom is knowing the difference.

Jesus often needs to remind us not to get in His way with how He deals with His maturing Bride. We have human pity and unsanctified mercy for those He is chastening. Those who are in a season of drawing apart, we seem to want them to get back into the rat race of the church. Be careful that you don't distract God's people with your opinions of what God is doing. He takes each of us into different seasons to make us like Him. **"Do not arouse or awaken love, until it** (she) **so desires."** He reminds the immature daughters of Jerusalem not to disturb her until she recognizes the new season of the Lord's dealings.

"By the gazelles and by the does of the fields." This speaks of the need for extra gentleness and sensitivity in relating to those who are immersed in a season of renewed intimacy. They must be allowed to draw near to God without our distractions.

The Royal Pair in Their Glorious Chariot

"Who is this?" In this season of increased intimacy her spiritual eyes opened to see Him in a new way. Perhaps in a vision or dream . . . the Holy Spirit asks her a question: **"Who is this coming up from the desert like a column of smoke. . . . "** The "desert" speaks of life on a fallen planet. Jesus Himself was once driven by the Spirit to the wilderness to be tested and proven faithful. Our King came out of His wilderness victorious. After the resurrection He entered the glory of God (a column of smoke) to sit on His throne.

Jesus is now a King that is no longer limited to His humanity in the wilderness. Clothed in splendor He came up out of this fallen world to re-enter the glory cloud of heaven. He is the Pillar of Cloud that comes up out of the desert!

The "smoke" speaks of the glory and majesty of God on display (Ex. 40:34, Rev. 15:8, Joel 2:28-30). Smoke is the result of the fire of the Holy Spirit burning up the sacrifices offered to Him. Who is this coming up out of the desert like a column of smoke? It is the Lord Jesus Christ coming through the clouds into the Seat of Honor. Now the bride has a vision of how marvelous He really is—a Wonderful, All-Powerful Savior. She will be safe in the desert with Him at her side.

"Perfumed with myrrh and incense . . . " The ascension of Jesus reveals both His suffering (myrrh) and His splendor (incense). As a burial spice, myrrh reminds us of the sacrifice of Jesus to redeem the Bride and purify her for Himself. Jesus is perfumed in myrrh. When He was on the cross carrying our sins He was drenched with myrrh. The sufferings were agony to Him, but they were perfume to the Father. The frankincense speaks of Jesus' intercession for the saints (Heb. 7:25). As Jesus ascended to the Father, He filled the golden bowl of incense with the fragrance of His intercession. What a merciful Friend He is!

"Made from all the spices of the merchant." The fragrance of the merchant is all over Jesus. Who is the merchant? Jesus is the Merchant who saw the pearl and sold all He had to claim the treasure of your love. You are His inheritance, His Bride. He bought you as a merchant would purchase the finest pearl. It cost Him His life to make you His Bride (Matt. 13:44-46). Sacred blood was shed for you. . . .

The Marriage Carriage

"Look! It is Solomon's carriage. . . . " The role of the Holy Spirit is to convince us that we are safe with Jesus. Many fear what it would cost to live for Jesus one hundred percent. Fear of missing out on the pleasures of life cause many to compromise. This is because we do not know how safe we are in His love. The lies of the enemy will always come with an accusation against Jesus. Can He be trusted? Will He be there? What if He lets you down or disappoints you? The devil's lies will produce fear.

Some people do not sever ungodly relationships because of the *fear* of being alone. Some do not tithe to the local church because they *fear* they will be left without adequate resources. Fear leads to compromise . . . always!

The Holy Spirit wants to show us the King's Glorious Nuptial Carriage. This is the wedding carriage or "palanquin," carried on the shoulders of His servants. In ancient times, Far Eastern brides were carried on men's shoulders in a sedan chair, referred to as a carriage. The Bride and Groom reclined within the veil, screened by curtains from public view. Bodyguards accompanied them as blazing torches lit up their pathway. This is the picture the Lord would show us of how we are carried through life in His covenant of grace.

We dwell with Him behind curtains. Like the Ark of Covenant, we are hidden with Him . . . concealed from the world and carried throughout life. Solomon's sumptuous carriage shows us how safe we are in the finished work of the cross where Jesus triumphed over all His foes. There is no safer place than to be with Him in His majestic carriage. If we are destined to sit with Him at His side enthroned as His Royal Queen (Rev. 19:6-7, Eph. 2:6), then this is our destiny, we will be kept safe in this age as His Bride-to-be! The chariot (carriage) of our Lord Jesus is a cloud of glory!

"Escorted by sixty warriors . . . " These warriors are the angels of God that surround us and minister to us (Heb. 1:14). This is extravagant protection. Presidents and statesmen only have 20-30 bodyguards around them at any one time . . . you have 60! Jesus is capable of keeping His Bride safe and protected. In the days of Solomon it was common for wedding parties to be ambushed and robbed, harming the royal family and stealing the gold and jewels. You will not be ambushed by the devil when you are riding with your King in His Royal Chariot. The Tabernacle in the wilderness had 60 strong poles to hold it up! Jesus has His noblest warriors surrounding you.

"All of them wearing the sword . . . prepared for the terrors of the night." None are novices; they are trained for war and prepared for any difficulty that might come. Intercessors are also like warriors with swords.

"King Solomon made for himself the carriage . . . " King Solomon, King of Israel, is a picture of the Lord Jesus. Jesus made the marriage carriage for Himself. Did you know that Jesus, the Creator, spoke into existence the tree that was fashioned into His cross? By His work on Calvary's cross, Jesus constructed a carriage that would express His love to the entire world. Our resting place is the cross; we are carried along in the safety of His cross.

"The wood from Lebanon" is a type of the humanity of Jesus. He descended from the ivory palaces (Ps. 45:8) to take on the flesh of man and partake of our human nature (symbolized by the wood). Wood from Lebanon was the most costly and fragrant wood. Jesus was like us. Yet, He is unlike us. He is the greatest of all, the Son of Man. Costly and fragrant was His sacrifice on a wooden cross for us. . . .

"Its posts he made of silver, its base of gold." The four pillars supporting the covering and curtains were made of silver—the symbol of redemption. Pillars of justice, power, love, and faithfulness provide our covering. The bottom of the carriage was made of gold. The foundations of our relationship are holy, pure, and divine. The silver and gold speak of Jesus Christ, who is both our Redeemer (silver) and our God (gold).

"Its seat was upholstered with purple, its interior lovingly inlaid by the daughters of Jerusalem." The upholstery of purple points to the royalty of the Lord Jesus, for a King wears purple. And what a purple this is . . . it represents the precious blood of Christ. We rest enthroned on a scarlet seat of royal authority, this chariot of salvation. We can rejoice without fear or doubt in the glory of the Cross. Jesus' blood has paid the price! The interior of this carriage is *"paved with love"* (KJV). There is a carpet of love surrounding the Lamb's wife. She is surrounded by priceless love . . . all love, nothing else but love. Those on the outside cannot fully appreciate what it is to be carried along under the love canopy.

Come and sit side by side with Jesus in His chariot of grace. Be carried with the One who carried your cross. What a soft and pleasant place to recline! Our Bridegroom finds rest in your love, even as you rest in His love. Although there are still many things wrong with the Bride, she is carried in the carriage of love. The affections of Jesus are the foundation of our relationship with Him, not our own feelings. Love brought Jesus to earth. Love led Him to the garden. Love took Him to the cross. Love brings Him to our hearts. Jesus and His fiancée will someday reign together from this purple throne. . . .

From *cedar*, to *silver*, to *gold*, to the *seat of purple*—the description advances step by step. Each phrase reveals more of the quality and preciousness of our salvation. As we go on with God, we discover more of the astounding glory of our salvation. Filled with new understanding, she exhorts others to gaze at the glory of the King, **"Come out . . . and look at King Solomon."**

The daughters of Jerusalem are now referred to as the **"daughters of Zion."** This is the spiritual term used for the people of God. Now the maiden is seeing the people with eyes of hope and love. Using the same method of encouragement toward the people as the King used with her, she prophesies of their growth in maturity. They will rise up to become the daughters of Zion who love the King. She points their gaze to the One wearing the crown.

The sovereignty and majesty of this King is now her theme. She wants them to see His authority over Satan, the world, and the nations. Your Beloved is the King wearing the Crown! When you see the crown you will not fear the mountains. When you see His true authority you will no longer fear the difficulties of life. **"The crown with which his mother crowned him on the day of his wedding . . . "** His mother speaks of the church. She says to others, "Come look at Him. See His royal authority. We have crowned Him with our love."

Jesus has worn the crown of glory from all eternity (Rev. 19:12). As King over many realms, He is to be honored, loved, and adored. But the crown He most longs for is the crown the church bestows upon Him on the day of His wedding. We will willingly submit our lives to Him in voluntary love . . . forever!

As the end-time Harvester, Jesus also wears the crown of our adoration as He reaps the nations of the earth.

I looked, and there before me was a white cloud, and seated on the cloud was one "like a son of man" with a crown of gold on his head and a sharp sickle in his hand. Then another angel came out of the temple and called in a loud voice to him who was sitting on the cloud, "Take your sickle and reap, because the time to reap has come, for the harvest of the earth is ripe." So he who was seated on the cloud swung his sickle over the earth, and the earth was harvested.

Revelation 14:14-16

As we glorify the Bridegroom and crown Him with our praises He is empowered to take the golden sickle and begin the great harvest of the nations.

Isaiah 62:5 states, *"As a bridegroom rejoices over his bride, so will your God rejoice over you."* We are the partners Jesus has longed for. On the day of His wedding His heart will burst with joy, for He will have you for Himself at last. Make His heart glad today . . . Just worship Him!

"How beautiful you are,
my darling!
Oh, how beautiful!"

Song of Songs 4:1
৪০৪৪

Affirmed by the King

Chapter 4:1-8
ಬಂಗ

*T*he Romance of Heaven is the theme of this inspired story. Jesus has found His "Princess Bride" and now He sweeps her off her feet! Like only this King could do, He speaks words of tender love to her. Words that wash over her soul . . . words of unconditional love. He speaks over her (and us!) words that inspire and prophesy of her destiny. . . .

The bride has yet to face the dark night she will experience in Chapter five. Knowing this, He speaks to her the words that will hold her fast in the time of trouble. . . . Drink deeply of the Words of your Lover-Friend, O maiden! You too, will need to draw strength through these words during the challenging seasons of life ahead. . . .

Another wave of Holy Love washes over the Bride, a love that will conquer her fear and her mistrust of the King. There is no scolding in the Song of Songs, only affirmation. We see the longing heart of God to be gracious (Isa. 30:18). It is astonishing every time we hear words like, **"How beautiful you are, My darling!"**

Can you see Jesus Christ standing before you this day saying those very words? He knows all about you and I, our stumbles and our tumbles—and still His thoughts are filled with love for each of us (Ps. 139:17-18). He has erased your sins, destroyed the evidence, deleted the files and washed you squeaky clean! He refuses to be your probation officer; He is your Savior! Jesus could bear your sins easier than He could bear your hopelessness. He loves you; He likes you; He adores you. He offered Sacred Blood to redeem you and make you part of His eternal Bride. As His Bride, His open heart of Love is revealed to you with indescribable joy, **"Oh, how beautiful, My Darling."**

We need to invent new words to even begin to describe God's love. We have a longing Father who waits to see us take one step back into His limitless, liberating love. The love of Jesus is not a temporary mood swing between His acts of judgment. His mercy endures forever. It endures past our failures, our immaturity, and our feeble attempts at walking with God. Our Abba is a Friend who calls us beautiful even when we are most aware of your weakness. His heart skips a beat when we draw near to Him even when our lives don't seem to work right.

We often see ourselves as shameful, unworthy of His affection. It becomes a mystery why He takes delight in us. It is time to hear Him sing His Song of Songs. This is the message that pierces our hearts with mercy. Loved in our immaturity; enjoyed by Him even while we have a hard time living with our self. What a King! What a Friend!

It must be repeated: This is the way God has chosen to change His weak, imperfect Bride. He washes her over and over again in cherishing love, removing the stain of sin from her soul (Eph. 5:29). The Holy Spirit will reveal the cherishing ministry of Jesus to the end-time church.

Many are the husbands who try to change their wives some other way (and the wives who attempt to change their husbands). It is only the power of love that breaks the power of inbred sin. The One who embraces us is stronger than the power of sin. His love breaks the stony heart to pieces, making us a responsive, tender Bride.

This is how He defines our life—not by our weak stumbles but by our desire to be a delight to Him. Jesus did not define the maiden by her lack of discipline, her heart of fear, and her momentary weakness. He knows the sincere desire in her spirit is to overcome these things and be fully His. He has read Chapter 8 already; He knows she will be leaning on Him.

The Bridegroom-King describes the Shulamite by the budding virtues coming forth, not the momentary failures of her life. He can see the awakened passions in our hearts even before they are fully walked out. God called Gideon a "mighty man of valor" while he was hiding in fear of the Midianites. God defines us by what we will be in the future. He sees destiny over you and describes you by that. He is a God who calls things forth before they "are;" this is His job description! (1:8,15,16; 2:10,13, 4:1,7,10; 6:4,10; 7:1) Jesus' beauty is reflected by those filled with His love.

End-time ministry in the church must follow the example set forth in this prophetic Masterpiece, the Song of Songs. Those entrusted with the care and nurture of the Bride must be affirmers, shapers of destiny, encouragers, and lovers of others. Saint-perfecters must be those who focus not on the inabilities and weaknesses of others, but on the budding virtues Jesus is bringing forth within. His *love* gets the job done, not angry exhortations.

Those who cooperate with Jesus in bringing forth the Radiant Bride will be gripped by the reality of His love. Jesus grows Christians by affirming them, not condemning them. Perhaps we could begin to follow the example of the One who has waited for all eternity for His cherished Bride. This is the strongest emotion in the heart of God. . . . Jesus has Holy love in His heart for you.

Jesus Prophesies of Her Maturity

The eight features of the maiden in this passage are pictures of the eight budding virtues that Jesus sees in His Bride.[1] He prophetically affirms her inward beauty with each description of her appearance. Jesus prophesies of the maturity that will arise in her and overcome the accusations of Satan. New Creation Life is coming forth within her as she becomes His crown of beauty.

"Your eyes behind your veil are doves. . . . " Her dove-like eyes refer to the "eyes" of her understanding (Eph. 1:18). Her heart is open to Him. She is "seeing" Him as He really is. The first thing Jesus honors is her perceptive eyes of faith. Her supernatural ability to perceive things is a part of her growth into maturity. The enemy seeks to "blind the eyes" of people to keep them from the riches of the gospel (II Cor. 4:4). Leah's eyes were "weak,"and she had limited spiritual insight (Gen. 29:17). It is with dove's eyes that the Shulamite maiden gazes on her King (Isa. 17:7).

The dove speaks of purity, loyalty and devotion.[2] Her eyes seek purity and look for goodness, not evil. Just as a dove's eye can only focus on one thing, her heart is single in focusing on Him . . . there could be none other (Matt. 6:21-23).

"Behind your veil" means that she is concealing her understanding behind the veil of humility. This is always a sign of true spiritual maturity. Many revelations and experiences in God are to grow us in faith and produce Christ-likeness within us. To prematurely share these experiences diminishes their power to deeply change us. Paul waited fourteen years before he shared what happened to him in a heavenly experience (II Cor. 12:1-9). True revelation, covered with humility, equals godly character. We must never take the "pearls" of true spiritual revelation and flippantly share with those who have no heart to receive it. Behind the veil is where the glory dwells. May we have dove's eyes behind our veil.

"Your hair is like a flock of goats. . . . " The hair is a symbol of devotion and consecration to God.[3] A "Nazarite" was one who was forbidden to cut his hair as an outward sign of their inward dedication to God (Num. 6:1-5). This was a part of a Nazarite's vow of separation to purity. Samson, a Nazarite, had long hair, which was the secret of his strength (Judges 16:17); and so it is with the Bride. A heart fully devoted to God will be strong and mighty for righteousness.

When the King notices her heart yielded in holy devotion, it moves Him. Her long hair is compared to a flock of goats that have descended from Mt. Gilead. Gilead was the place where the sheep and goats were kept, awaiting sacrifice in the temple. The sacrificial lambs grazed on Mt. Gilead. Jesus extols her dedication comparing it to a goat coming from the mountain ready for sacrifice. She becomes a *"living sacrifice"* by her response to the mercies of God (Rom. 12:1). Like a dedicated offering is her heart of devotion. How strong has her love become for her God! Beloved, keep your vows of devotion to Jesus and display His love to the world.

"Your teeth are like a flock of sheep. . . . " The teeth indicate her ability to eat the strong meat given to her from the Word of God. She has matured enough to chew the solid truths of the Word of God (Heb. 5:13-14). Infants have no teeth to chew their food (I Cor. 3:1-3). They are not yet able to acquire God's teachings as *revelation*. We have an abundance of food to eat in the Bible, but few of us have the ability to digest it and make it our own. The

Bride now has the capacity to take in the deeper truths of God (John 5:39-40).

"Like a flock of sheep just shorn." God designates sheep as clean animals in the Old Testament. To "shear the sheep" is to take off the excess "wool" of fleshly zeal. The removal of the excess wool speaks to us of the energy of the flesh that must be left behind when you move into the Holy Place (Ezek. 44:17). There is to be no sweat in God's presence. Priests of God are instructed not to wear wool so they won't sweat as they serve the Lord. The flesh doesn't need to work harder to please God; it needs to be shorn!

Have you been sheared lately? Isn't it time for a buzz cut, lambs of God! Jesus sees His Bride as one who has been delivered from "sweating it out" in striving to serve Him. Many of us need to be shorn of the wisdom of the world and renewed in our minds. Striving in the flesh will bring a curse of barrenness (Jer. 17:5-6). The maiden's devotion (hair) is like a flock of sheep just shorn. She has digested the Word and knows that spiritual growth is not by her power and zeal alone, but by the reality of the Scriptures lived out daily.

"Coming up from the washing." The washing of the Word has cleansed her heart (Eph. 5:25-26 & James 1:21). Cleansed from impure fleshly motives, she has taken the Word and made it her own. As we receive the Word and meditate upon it, our minds are washed and renewed. Her mind has been transformed, sanctified and cleansed by receiving the words of God.

"Each has its twin; not one of them is alone." These "twins" speak of the balance of wisdom; she holds on to old truths as she reaches for the new. Balanced and beautiful, she is capable of handling truth in its many-sided features. The bearing of twins also speaks of *fruitfulness* . . . the double blessing!

"Your lips are like a scarlet ribbon . . . " The lips are what is used when we communicate. The communication of her mouth reveals what is deep in her heart. Her speech has taken on the "scarlet" qualities of redemption as she uses words to bless, not wound others. She is even able to gently respond to those who oppose her (II Tim. 2:24-26, Prov. 15:1). Her words have now become lovely, no longer speaking vain or foolish things. Her lips are like a *scarlet* cord.[4]

The maiden is now using her speech to redeem and rescue the immature and perishing. Edifying speech releases grace to others (Col. 4:6). As we grow in the virtues of Christ, our words will become like "apples of gold in settings of silver" (Prov. 25:11). We treat others and speak of them with redeeming mercy. When our lips are purged then we are mature and ready to be a "sent one" for the Lord to use (Isa. 6:1-6, James 2:3).

The theme of mercy must be heard from our lips to the despised and bruised of the world. Do your words release grace to others or do they scorch and sear the heart? Have your words been washed in the scarlet flow of redemption? Just as the scarlet thread of Rahab brought redemption to her house, the lips of the Bride will bring redemption and deliverance to the hurting. May we have lips that always find redeeming qualities in others — even those who speak evil of us.

In the beginning, she had asked for the kisses of His mouth. Now He says of His maturing Bride, **"Your mouth is lovely."** She has the capacity to share intimacy with her Beloved. Her lips refer to her speech, but the mouth is related to the sweet kisses of worship and adoration that she brings to Him. He finds intimacy with her as He shares His secrets; it is lovely in His sight. Jesus is delighted with the communion they now share.

"Your temples ... like the halves of a pomegranate ... "
The temples or "cheeks" speak of her emotions. From her countenance she displays the emotions of her heart.[5] As Jesus looks behind her veil He sees that the emotions of her heart are toward Him. Her rosy cheeks are like the sweet red fruit of a pomegranate. The Lord finds pleasure in her as her heart has opened up to Him. She is sensitive to shameful things (red from blushing).

All of these emotions are seen **"behind your veil."** Her modesty and hidden life before God makes her attractive. She is displaying great tenderness to Him without boasting or displaying before others. Carved on the very top of the pillars in Solomon's temple were rows of pomegranates (I Kings 7:20 & Rev. 3:12). As the Lord looked down from on high to see His "Temple" he saw pomegranates opened up before Him. May our lives be laid open moment by moment to the gaze of Jesus Christ. Lord, make our opened hearts a constant delight to you!

"Your neck is like the tower of David. . . . " The neck represents the will. Those stubborn and proud of heart are called "stiff-necked." Those with a yielded will, often bow their necks (heads) in humility and submission. Conquering kings would put their feet upon the necks of their enemies to show that they had prevailed over them. The maiden's will, yielded to the King is a beautiful feature of the maturing Bride of Christ. Her neck (compared to a high tower) speaks of an upright will that is determined to do the right thing ... no matter what the cost.

She is no longer double-minded. He tells her, "You are standing on solid spiritual ground with a resolute will to fulfill my destiny for you. I can see you will not be turned aside to lesser pursuits." Her will is now like the heart of David (Ps. 57:7).

Like David did, she has resolutely fixed her will to go after her Beloved. David's tower was a place where the weapons of warfare were stored.[6] The Shulamite's voluntary decision to follow the King is like a storehouse of mighty weapons against the opposition of Satan. He views her inward life and resolute will as an armory full of offensive weapons. Nehemiah referred to an armory near the king's tower (Neh. 3:19,25).

"On it hang a thousand shields, all of them shields of warriors." This armory has one thousand shields of the mightiest warriors hanging upon it. The number one thousand speaks of abundant protection and strength against the enemy. She is taking captive every thought and bringing it into obedience to Christ (II Cor. 10:5). The shields of skilled warriors who have been proven in battle could refer to the testimony throughout church history of those servants of Christ who have finished their course faithfully to the end (Heb. 11:32-40). She has learned from their witness and example. Our resolute faith is that mighty shield, preserving us in every battle (Eph. 6:16).

"Your breasts are like . . . fawns of a gazelle . . . " The breasts speak of nourishment for the babes, the newborn. Like a nursing mother the church will give sustenance to her young. But what kind of life substance will she impart? Gentleness, innocence and purity— **"like fawns, like twin[7] fawns of a gazelle."**

She is releasing the right kind of life to those who are led to the Savior. Like twin fawns of a gazelle that have fed on lilies (purity of heart) she is able to multiply a double-portion to those she has touched. Her sacred affections are pure and imparted to the young and immature. She has fed herself properly among those pure of heart and is quite able to nurture others.

"Putting on faith and love as a breastplate" (I Thess. 5:8). Faith and love are the qualities seen in her life as the maturing Bride. Faith and love combined form righteousness before God and men. These enduring traits of Christlikeness are now developed and affirmed from Jesus to His church. Not only is she growing in maturity, but she is able to nourish and impart life to others.

She Says "Yes" to the Cross

"I will go to the mountain of myrrh. . . . " After hearing these eight prophetic affirmations over her life, she is now willing to leave her comfort zone. She is ready to leave the predictable place from behind her wall and go the mountaintops. She has learned much; now her heart is prepared for the high places of warfare and intercession. The Bride is ready to be trained and discipled for the King!

At this point in the Song, the maiden from Shunem makes a life changing decision. From this point forward, she will never be the same. His love has conquered her. His eyes of passion for her have melted away the fear of the high places. She arises with fresh determination to pay the price and go to the mountain of myrrh. The combination of His discipline (3:1-5), the new revelation of how safe He really is (3:6-11), and His undying love expressed to her has melted her heart. Now she is ready for the mountains. Every fear in her heart has been removed; she will arise and go!

This was the challenge she said "No" to earlier. Jesus is so wise and capable of changing our hearts. So often we resist the challenges of spiritual growth, only later to say "yes" and take His hand. Real change in our life does not come by gritting our teeth but by falling in love. His affection for us breaks the power of a thousand sins. He is preparing you and I for the high place and for greater degrees of spiritual warfare.

But what really are we saying yes to? Do we even know what it means to go with Him? To go to the **"mountain of myrrh"** is to embrace the cross; the death of selfishness within. . . . He stands as One who leaps over mountains saying, "Arise and Come!"

It is time to embrace the Cross unto self-denying love, as we pour out our lives for the nations." To say "yes" to the mountain of myrrh is a lifetime commitment to embrace the Cross. There is a life principle that the end-time Bride will understand; it is the reality of the Cross. More than an event, or an emblem, it is the Tree of Life, Jacob's Ladder and the Burning Bush. To the mountain of myrrh every seeking heart will go . . . and it is there we find Him. This is where we are taught the ways of God and where we discover self-abandonment. *We* must learn the same lesson that the maiden learned. The days when we only sought our own pleasure are over when we choose to be a faithful Bride.

The **"hill of incense"** is the place of abandoned intercession and worship. A hill is smaller than a mountain. It is the hill of incense that enables us to scale the mountain of myrrh. Every passionate believer must learn the lessons of self-abandoned worship and intercession. None of us are sufficient to scale mountains and run with Jesus without a life of prayer. Our incense is our prayers to God before His throne (Rev. 5:8, Ps. 141:2). This is true communion with God in the heavenlies while we embrace a life of self-denial on earth.

"Until the Day breaks and the shadows flee." The Day is the time of total victory over darkness. She makes the inner vow that she will go with Jesus to the place of the Cross until all her dark shadows have fled, until all of her imperfections have been removed by the light of His

Day. She will live with Him on the hill of incense and the mountain of myrrh until all her compromises have been dealt with in His Glorious Presence. She will continue on the mountain of myrrh while cultivating a life of intercession on the hill of frankincense. This is where the Bride begins to emerge without spot and without wrinkle. The greater anointing found on the mountain of myrrh will accomplish this.

What will His response be to all this? Her decision to run with Him brought forth a fresh affirmation: **"All beautiful you are, my darling; there is no flaw in you."** Can you imagine hearing Jesus say this to you today? You are altogether ravishing to His heart! He speaks again of her inward beauty coming forth. She is His darling, His lover-friend. Not, "you will be," but "you are" right now . . . even before you ascend the hill of the Lord. All He sees in her is the beauty of her abandonment to Him.

Her whole life is summed up in these words, **"There is no flaw in you."** This doesn't mean she is without sin, for she has not yet passed the ultimate test she is to endure in Chapter 5. Yet her willingness to embrace the cross and run with Him has delighted His heart. Jesus sees in her an undying desire to take all that He will teach her and walk in the light she has found in Him. Perfect love has begun to cast out her fear. . . .

"Come with Me. . . . " The King invites her to come into intimate partnership with Him, to look at the nations from His point of view. She is now being discipled in the heavenly perspective of what God wants to do among the people of the earth. In the high place she can see what was had confused her in the past. This is an invitation for her to be taught lessons of higher levels of spiritual warfare and be equipped to sit as a Bride at His side. Lebanon's peaks, where the lions and leopards roam, are the places of advanced spiritual warfare. Now she ascends with Him to engage in active service and partnership with Jesus.[8]

Now He calls her **"My Bride."** This is the first reference to her as the Bride of Christ in the book. She has come forth from her darkness to skip with Him on mountains. This shows that she truly has bridal affection for the Son of God. Her passion for Him has taken her to the Cross and a life of intercession. As His beautiful Bride they take a journey together to the high place and view the world from His perspective as eternal Partners! In the final hours of the church age, it will be the Spirit and the Bride that says, "Come!" This Bridal Cry will intensify until our passion is to know Him as Husband (Hos. 2:16).

To be called His Bride means that all the privileges of the relationship become ours. To be called His spouse, His cherished one . . . even when we can still remember all the times we fought Him and His perfect will for our lives. We are heirs of all things when we become His Bride. Everything He has is now ours. Our poverty is drowned out in the riches of His redeeming love.

Although a picture of spiritual warfare, Lebanon's mountains were also known for their breathtaking beauty (Lebanon = "snowy mountain"). The glory of Lebanon is mentioned in Isaiah 35:2. Jesus' countenance is like Lebanon (Song of Songs 5:15, Hos. 14:6). Moses longed to see Lebanon (Deut. 3:25). Solomon built a summer home in Lebanon because of its forests. This view from the high place is symbolic of where we have already been seated with Christ (Eph. 2:6, Col. 3:1-4). She must now focus on the eternal, what is unseen, rather than merely the natural world (II Cor. 4:8, 5:7). It is time for the Bride to look from the top of the mountain.

"The crest of Amana (*seal of covenant*), **the top of Senir** (*glistening peak*), **the summit of Hermon** (*high, majestic*)."** These are the realms of the spirit where true realities are understood. These are the highest peaks that give view to the land of Promise. Many of the saints have stood on these high peaks to look into the realm God is about to release to the earth. The end-time church will be given startling revelations that have been undisclosed until now (Dan. 12). Israel had to conquer Amorite kings before they could scale this mountain range, a picture of the flesh being subdued and broken before revelation comes.

"From the lion's dens and the mountain haunts of the leopards." Lions and leopards are the spiritual forces of evil that roam in the high place (Eph. 6:12). Satan is called a roaring lion, seeking to devour through fear (I Pet. 5:7-8). Now the maiden is taking her place at the King's side as He wars against demonic principalities in the Devil's hideout (Hab. 2:17, Ps. 57:4). To face him with holy power we must daily embrace the Cross . . . even when forgotten by others.

The Shulamite said YES!

---

1. He gives her a new identity (eight = new beginning) so she will grow into it.
2. The Holy Spirit Himself is seen in Scripture as a Dove (Matt. 3:16).
3. Goat hair was used to construct the curtains of the Tabernacle - the place where those separated to God would commune with Him.
4. The scarlet cord that Rahab placed outside her wall was a picture of the blood of Christ and His redeeming love. (See Joshua 2.)
5. Sadness, joy, anger, frustration, etc. are all emotions that are seen on the countenance. Godly emotions can be greatly used by God.
6. Solomon, David's son, knew very well about his father's armory.
7. The two breasts also point us to the Law and the Prophets, the Old and New Testaments, Christ's mercy and truth.
8. This is really where He wanted to take her in 2:10-13.

*"You have stolen my heart
with one glance of your eyes. . . . "*

Song of Songs 4:9
෫ඏൽ

The Ravished Heart of God

Chapter 4:9–5:1

ဆေ CB

$\mathcal{J}$esus, the King of all the ages, unveils His heart of love to the maiden. For all eternity He has longed for a Bride, a partner to sit with Him on His throne. Now He tells her just what He thinks of her. Beloved, *YOU* are the one He speaks to like this. Can't you hear Him telling you that you have conquered His heart? It is true . . . you are the one He came to save. . . .

The world has yet to see the fiery passion that Jesus has for His Bride. Her love has simply ravished His heart. She has said "yes" to the Mountains of Myrrh, she is willing to embrace the cross. It's as though He can see the fear in her eyes, so the King reassures her in love. *"You will be safe, dear one. Every time you glance at Me, my heart skips a beat."* Have you ever wondered how Jesus really feels about you? These verses give us an answer few are prepared to handle. . . .

Jesus wants to reveal His passion and enjoyment of *you.* He wants to describe how you have thrilled His heart. The Creator of emotions wants to show His emotions toward you. Get ready to receive the most astonishing love from the very heart and lips of Jesus Christ. *Your worship makes His heart beat faster.*

Imagine . . . the heart of God ravished over you. *Right now!* Not just later when you live better. In the mess of life, Jesus is completely overjoyed with you.

This phrase **"You have stolen my heart,"** can be translated, "You have made my heart skip a beat!" "You have enchanted, enthralled my heart!" "You have brought ecstasy to my heart!" Or, "You have made my heart swell with joy." Need He say more?

Jesus' heart is filled with an extravagant, furious love that can never be quenched. His loving affection for His people can barely be described. He is overcome with emotions of joy and delight every time you come to His mind (all the time!).

We struggle with people, but Jesus finds the same people we struggle with, unusually attractive. His heart is captivated with love for human beings even while they are insecure, weak, and imperfect. This is the love of Jesus that will demolish strongholds of rejection and the negative thoughts that are entrenched in human hearts. Nothing is more powerful than omnipotent love. His passion for you is all consuming, relentless.

The same way the Father loves the Son is the way Jesus loves you. *"As the Father has loved Me, so have I loved you"* (John 15:9). Sooner or later it will dawn on you; God could not love you any more than He does right now! If you are better tomorrow, He will not love you more. If you are worse tomorrow, He will not love you any less. The "tractor beam" of Divine Love has captured us. . . . **"You have stolen my heart!"**

Our hearts must be able to rest in the undisturbed love of Jesus, or the shaking around us will affect the sweet communion of our hearts with Him. It is not enough that we understand what He did on the cross or what He will do in the coming revival. We must know about His deepest desires for us and how He feels about us now. This gives us insight into His personality and why He does what He does. Discipled in love, we will not be moved or shaken.

Others are not as kind as Jesus. Only the Son of God can see loveliness in you and I when others see our grime. Jesus wears grace glasses. As God sees you growing and fulfilling your purpose in life, joy floods His heart. Your glance of love is what He died for. Keep looking at Jesus until you hear Him say, **"With one glance of your eyes you have stolen My heart."**

Jesus cannot resist one look from the eyes of one who is sincere in seeking Him. Lift up your eyes to Him today. Why are you so downcast? One glance from your eyes and you have ravished the heart of the Son of God. It is not the gifted ones who have stolen His heart, it is the yielded ones. . . .

We do not really understand what our worship does to the heart of Jesus Christ. One translation reads: "With one glance of your eyes you have given Me courage." Beloved, hear this prophetic word over you:

Let Me tell you what you mean to Me, My Beloved Bride. Every time you look at Me in worship and adoration, you capture My heart! You enflame My heart when you look to Me out of your place of pain and isolation. . . . I am energized once again to perfect your love and change you into My image. One glance from your eyes does to Me what the armies and kings could not do; you have conquered Me fully. I will give you all that I have to make you my Partner, My Bride. I am for you. You are willing to learn the lessons of the dark trails on the mountain of myrrh. I turn to you, even as you turn to Me. Your thoughts of Me, your prayers to Me in the night seasons, your love and obedience to Me have become delightful — more than wine! Pursue me even if

*you don't sense that I am near. Come . . . seek for Me. I
will be found by you, My Bride!*

Our Love-Partnership

"Sister" speaks of being of like nature; from the
same family (Heb. 2:10-18, Matt. 12:49-50). How incredible and humbling that Jesus would take our nature upon
Himself, and by the Resurrection give us His! He is not
ashamed to call us brother/sister. He calls us part of His
family, claiming for Himself a relationship with us in the
family of grace.

More than a King, He is a brother. Did you know
your Brother is a King? **"Bride"** or spouse reveals our call
to be His partners, co-heirs of all things at the side of Jesus
for all eternity. Jesus loves His Bride. You are His nearest
and dearest. . . .

"With one jewel of your necklace . . . " The necklace
speaks of her submitted will to the purpose of God. It is
easy to say that we are willing, but what happens when
He wants us to do what we don't want to do? When we
say "yes" to God it is a jewel on our necklace. When we
touch His authority and say "yes" we become one who
has stolen His heart.

Every sincere response to Jesus is another link of
gold, a precious jewel upon our neck. His heart is thrilled
over every response of tenderness to Him. Weak human
beings that say "yes" to Him so easily conquer Jesus.

How Jesus Views Your Love For Him

**"How delightful is your love, how much more pleas-
ing is your love than wine."** These are the words she used
in speaking to Him. Now He turns to her and says, "*Your
love is more pleasing to Me than anything else in the creat-*

ed universe." It is true. My cold, feeble love is precious to the Lord Jesus. He calls my love for Him delightful. Jesus values your love more than any other pleasure there is. He measures it not by its strength, but by its sincerity. He knows you love Him although you fail and sin. Even feeble love gladdens the heart of the Son of God.

You are His banqueting table. Your heart is a love feast for Jesus. When you long for Him and are drawn by Bridal affection into the waves of worship—you are delightful to the Son of God! Beautiful and pleasing are your ways when you pour out pure worship to Him. He desires love more than your sacrificial works of ministry (Hos. 6:7, I Cor. 13:3, Rev. 2:1-5).

The love of all the angels combined cannot be compared to your love poured out to Him. All the joys of paradise are nothing to the joys He experiences in spending time with you. Have you ever wondered how Jesus feels about your prayers? I bet you think your prayer life stinks . . . right? But Jesus says it smells like perfume . . . **"the fragrance of your perfume."** Our intercession and weak worship is a fragrant perfume to the King.

Jesus is saying to you, "Your love is my wine. Your virtues are my sweet smelling perfume." She has spent so much time with Him that she now smells like Him. His fragrance is upon her. How incredible to think that we are able to minister to Him, to delight His heart.

Paul mentions the fragrance as the sweet aroma of Christ that comes forth from the redeemed (II Cor. 2:14-16). This was written to one of the most messed up churches in the New Testament—Corinth. To God, our devotional life is more pleasing than any spice, regardless of what we think is lacking.

Rare and exquisite spices were exchanged as gifts among royalty. The Queen of Sheba gave spices as a gift to Solomon (I Kings 10:2). Wise men brought spices to Jesus at

His birth for they knew He was a King (Matt. 2:11). These same spices were also included in the sacred anointing oil (Ex. 30:23-24). Our love for Jesus, our prayers to Him, our weak worship, our thoughts toward Him—they all blend to form the finest fragrance of sacred devotion to the Lord.

Your King notices your every word. . . . He hears the sigh of your heart as you lean toward Him. **"Your lips drop sweetness as the honeycomb. . . . "** The lips, of course, refer to our speech (See notes on 4:3.). The words that the Bride speaks to God and to others are like sweet honey. Jesus notices every word that comes from the lips of His Bride. *"Pleasant words are a honeycomb, sweet to the soul and healing to the bones"* (Prov. 16:24).

Her lips drop sweetness, in contrast to gushing sweetness. Just the right amount of honey in her speech brings sweetness to the soul. *"The tongue of the wise commends knowledge, but the mouth of the fool gushes folly"* (Prov. 15:2).

"Milk and honey are under your tongue." These are the two foods given to babes. The Bride is now nourishing others with loving words. Milk and honey also characterize the abundance of the Promised Land. There is an abundance of kindness and wisdom in all that she spoke. "Under your tongue" means that her heart and her words are in agreement. Her private thoughts are pondered in her heart before she speaks them. She holds them under her tongue with honey and cream. The lips and tongue are the channel of her ministry; her speech has changed.

"The fragrance of your garments . . . " Her garments refer to acts of service that she performs out of love for the King (Rev. 19:6-8). Every deed of humble service, regardless of how insignificant it may seem to you, will not go unnoticed by the King (Heb. 6:10). Jesus views her everyday ministry as fragrant, carrying the aroma of His life.

Paul spoke of the offerings to his ministry from the church at Philippi as a fragrant aroma of the sacrifice of Christ, pleasing to God. Jesus sees your devoted deeds and calls them good and pure. The garments of royal ministry are upon you.

You smell good to Jesus. The garlic smell of Egypt has been replaced by the fragrance of a forest in Lebanon. When you put on Christ as your robe of righteousness, His life covers you in His glorious aroma.

His Private Paradise

The heart of the Bride is the private paradise of King Jesus. An enclosed garden would be used only for the King—a place for His pleasure, for His enjoyment. Once she was a wilderness overgrown with weeds, but now she is His fruitful garden. **"You are a garden locked up, My sister, My Bride. . . . "**

It is said that King Solomon had an enclosed garden that he would often retreat to for solitude and rest. Beloved, you are a garden that has only one use—to bring pleasure to your Creator. This garden is not a place of agriculture, but a place of fellowship and communion. God placed man and woman in a garden as a picture of what our relationship with Him is to be (I Cor. 3:6-9).

Our hearts must be His enclosed Eden. With a gate locked to the world, reserved for the King. Our inner castle, where we dwell in His chambers, must be kept locked for His use only. Our imaginations and fantasies must be of our beautiful Lord Jesus. The enemy will come to ruin that serene place, but he must be kept out at the locked gate—where only purity can enter.

God told Cain that,*"sin lies at the door."* Jesus told His church, *"Behold I stand at the door and knock."* Both sin and Jesus want to enter our hearts. When we see ourselves as

His **"garden locked up,"** only our Lord Jesus will enter. Out of this garden-relationship will flow true life and ministry bearing fruit for His glory. The Bride is a garden locked up and sealed. His very glory is all around her. Jesus' Bride is not open to sin but is protected from the devil—enjoyed exclusively by Jesus. God will help us live in this truth if we really seek it.

There is a place in God where temptation will not overcome you (I Cor. 10:13). Jesus really can keep us from falling (Jude 24). Our inner wilderness can become His Eden, the garden of the Lord. No one can plunder His locked garden . . . He alone holds the key.

"You are a spring enclosed. . . . " This fresh water spring is what waters the King's garden. He compares her to a private spring that is not polluted; it is a covered spring that cannot be defiled by unclean things. She is not a watering hole for wild animals that would muddy the spring, but a drinking fountain for her Beloved.

The Bride does not want to be polluted by the things of this world; she is reserved for the King. Her clean life brings refreshing to His heart. Out of her inner being flows this living water. Your secret thoughts and meditations are like cool streams of water to your King.

> *The Lord will guide you always; He will satisfy your needs in a sun-scorched land and will strengthen your frame. You will be a well-watered garden, like a spring-whose waters never fail.*

> Isaiah 58:11

"A sealed fountain . . . " She is His bubbling spring, His sacred fountain, hidden from public use. Jesus Himself drinks from this cistern (Prov. 5:15). There is a legend that King Solomon had a secret sealed fountain known only to him. He had it sealed in such a way that only with his signet ring could it be opened up to flow.

The doors of the secret spring would open up releasing sweet waters of which no one could drink except he. We have become Jesus' holy and sacred fountain, sealed by the Holy Spirit (Eph. 4:30).

He knows the pathway into your spirit and with His touch (kiss) the fountains flow within. Jesus knows what melody moves you. Your heart melts when He sings His Song over you.

"Your plants are an orchard of pomegranates. . . . " Her mind has become an orchard of pomegranates, a paradise of godly thoughts. The church is like an orchard, full of pleasant fruits, with diverse plants and spices. We are not a barren wilderness. Jesus gazes at His Bride and views us as the most pleasant fruitful garden filled with many trees and plants. We are each one a delight to Him with our different gifts and expressions of worship.

The pomegranate is a sweet fruit that must be broken open to eat. When we are broken open to God, our ministry becomes sweet to Him and to others. The pomegranate is a symbol of pure and golden thoughts in the Bride's heart open to Him. This choice fruit is a delight to others as she impacts the nations with the fruits of a yielded life (Isa. 51:3).

She is now filled with the fragrance of His love, His joy, His peace (Gal. 5:22-23). The nine fruits of the Spirit are coming out of her personality as the King shines forth. **"An orchard . . . choice fruits . . . every kind . . . all the finest . . . "** Rare and exquisite spices are coming forth as the beauty of her devoted heart is revealed. She has become a fruit-filled garden full of delight and pleasure for the King. By dwelling on the Word she is constantly filled with His life.

These exotic fruits and spices have to be imported; they came from another land. The heavenly life of the

Spirit is now blooming within as symbolized by these 9 spices and flowers. . . .

Henna

Henna comes from a tree whose leaves yield a fluid used as red dye. The primary root word for henna means "to forgive." It signifies the shed blood of the cross—the costly work of God that has brought the Bride into the fragrance of Christ. The maiden had used henna blossoms to describe the Lord (1:14); now He uses the same term to describe her inward life. He recognizes His likeness sprouting forth in her.

In the ancient Jewish tradition, the night before the wedding, the bride's hands and feet are stained with henna. The Bride of the crucified Lamb is to exude the sweet smell of forgiveness in her works (hands) and her walk (feet). We are to be those who continually release forgiveness and mercy to others.

Nard

Nard is the spikenard that Mary poured on the feet of Jesus (John 12:3). Pure nard is an extremely costly spice. It is taken from the dried stems of a plant that grows high in the Himalayas, where the sun is strong and pure.

The Hebrew root of nard is "light." Jesus Christ is the True Light, in Him there is no darkness (I John 1:5). The Bride must live as one with Him in perfect light—nothing hidden, nothing of shadows. We are to be those lampstands in His Holy Place.

Eventually, even our shadows will be so infused with light from God that the sick will be healed when we walk by them (Acts 5:15). The maiden first smelled this spikenard as she sat at the King's table of abundance (1:12). Our worship is the sweetest perfume to the nostrils of our King.

Saffron

Saffron is the crocus, the lover's perfume, costly and fragrant. The Shulamite adores the Son of God. Saffron can also mean a yellowish orange—the gold of His character is shining on her walk. Saffron is a costly and valuable spice that is literally worth its weight in gold.

Faith is also so valuable; " . . . *so that your faith — of greater worth than gold . . . may be proved genuine and may result in praise, glory and honor when Jesus Christ is revealed."*

The faith of Jesus was proved genuine in every testing He endured. This golden faith has now been given to you as the sweetest spice in your heart.

Calamus

Calamus is taken from a marsh plant known as "sweet flag," that produces a fragrant oil. The Hebrew word for this spice means "erect or upright." God's poetic name for Israel was "Jeshurun" which means "upright one" (Isa. 44:2). Jesus is the True Upright One. As His chosen ones, we are to walk in righteousness and be upright in His grace (Isa. 26:7).

Cinnamon

Cinnamon emits a fragrance that is representative of an odor of holiness to the Lord. This was used in the sacred anointing oil of the priests and Tabernacle. It was one of the holy ingredients used to set apart those called to Divine service. Our consecration to Christ is to be like "cinnamon" to Him and to the world.

Every Kind of Incense Tree

Every kind of incense tree speaks of the fragrant cedars or trees of frankincense. They represent the purity of devotion of the resurrected Christ as He intercedes before the Father. His prayers rise like incense to the throne of grace. Our Lord Jesus is set apart to this wonderful ministry of intercession night and day. As our Magnificent Intercessor, He releases the Spirit of Grace and Supplication in our lives.

The soothing aroma of a life filled with God is now being released from the Bride. Every variety of frankincense is pouring forth from her. These trees had to be cut to give forth their fragrance, just as the Bride must be broken before the fragrance of Jesus spills forth.

Myrrh

Myrrh is the suffering fragrance that constantly reminds the maiden of the costly sacrifice of Jesus on the Cross. The spice of myrrh comes from the pierced bark of a thorny tree. What a clear picture of the cross and sufferings of our Lord Jesus. He was a Son that learned obedience from the things that He suffered (Heb. 5:8). Jesus emptied Himself of His own will and joyfully came to earth, knowing what was awaiting Him. Each believer is likewise called to exude this fragrance of a heart walking in full obedience to Christ by denying our own self life. When we walk through every valley with Jesus we are entering into "the fellowship of His sufferings" (Phil. 3:10).

Aloes & All the Finest Spices

Aloes are considered by many as the *healing balm*. The presence of the Lord within her is now released as healing balm to those she touches. Jesus' robes smelled of aloes (Ps. 45:8). One of the names used by some for aloes is the "Eagle Wood." Like eagles, we fly above our wounds, free from the past as we walk in intimacy with Him. Loving the Bridegroom heals the heart (Rom. 8:28).

All the finest spices—The word "finest" can mean chief or head spices. Jesus is the Head of the Church who has shared His finest spices with the Bride. These are all the symbols of the rarity and beauty of the maiden.

His Sanctuary

She is His Garden of Eden, His Sanctuary! His love has built a wall around her; no one else can have her. **"You are a garden fountain, a well of flowing water. . . . "** Other translations render this: "You are a fountain of gardens, a well of living water." She is His Sanctuary from which the River of Life is flowing (Ezek. 47:12). Jesus prophesied that *"streams of living water will flow from within"* (John 7:37-38). She has an inward source of supply and grace. As His fountain, she springs up with fresh zeal and affection for Him.

Notice the progression in this verse: A fountain, a well, a stream. The well is deep and only Jesus can draw the water forth. A well stores water which can be drawn forth when needed. A well supplies refreshment in dry seasons. So is the inner being of the one in love with Jesus. Her past life of seeking God is now paying off; a well has been dug. The overflow of His life will break forth spontaneously within those who are renewed in spirit.

The streams of Lebanon are a picture of the outward graces that are shared as refreshment for others. She is not a creek or brook, she is a flowing stream—an abundance of grace is in her. Lebanon is a lofty peak that speaks of the true source of these blessings—the heavenly places. Out of communion with Christ, streams and rivers flow to bless others. . . .

She Cries For Increased Anointing!

The Shulamite has heard these words from the Lord. She knows now that she is His garden of delight, His Garden of Eden. The words spoken to the maiden were a declaration of confidence from her Lover prompting her to cry for the north wind. The King knew just what she needed to become more anointed as His vessel of grace.

Within her blooms the fruits and spices of a life yielded to Him. The water of life is flowing from her inner being. She flings her arms wide open and bursts forth with, **"Awake, north wind, and come, south wind! Blow on my garden, that its fragrance may spread abroad."**

This is an incredible cry coming from her heart. She asks for the breath of heaven to stir her garden and unlock the fragrances in her heart. Looking away from herself she begins to prophesy to the winds to begin to stir her life. The north wind is the cold, biting wind of adversity. . . . Does she really want the north wind to blow upon her heart?

She is willing to embrace difficult circumstances if they will make fruit grow and His fragrance spread. She cries for the *north wind* to be awakened and do its work in her soul. Have you been "blown away" yet?

With an unexpected fierceness, the north wind will one day blow upon every passionate heart. There are some issues of God's training in our lives that can only result from testing and trials. Watchman Nee has said, "We never learn anything new about God except by adversity."

Deep pockets of unperceived pride, self-confidence, anger, and fear will only be exposed by the cold and cutting blast of the north winds. The Shulamite now understands the importance of adversity in the process of maturing into a fragrant garden for God. She cries out for more discipline, more training, more hardship. . . . " *Whatever it takes to make me like You, Lord!* Awaken north wind! Come do your work in me! Blow on my garden! Blow on my ministry! Blow on my life in you! Finish the work of bringing forth Your life in me."

It was the north wind that broke Mary's alabaster box and released the fragrance of her garden throughout the house. Humbling our heart in repentance and brokenness will release His fragrance . . . but so often we are unwilling to go there.

We must ask the Lord to send us *anything* that will release Kingdom life in us. The Lord will someday bring you to the place in your relationship with Him where external circumstances are not your delight, but the Lord Himself will be your joy and strength. This is the heritage of the servants of the Lord. Cry for the north wind!

What about the *"south wind?"* This is the mild breeze of refreshing—the cool breeze of grace that blesses and caresses. It is Divine love warming her heart. She asks for the Comforter to come. She realizes that it takes both adversity and blessing to bring the aroma of Christ from within her.

Ezekiel prophesied to the winds to blow, and life came into dry bones. When the winds blow, when His breath blows upon her garden, all that is dead within her springs to life. At times, the north wind and south wind will blow all at once in order to swiftly mature us and release divine fragrance from our garden.

The goat-keeping maiden is truly becoming like the One she loves. What matters most to her is that her garden-perfume **"may spread abroad."** The wind that blows on her garden is the breath of the Lord bringing grace and equipping mercy.

"Wind" and "breath" are the same word in Hebrew. There is a blow and a flow. Her desire is to have a life filled with God's power and anointing, filled so completely that others smell Him.

His Garden

For the first time in the book of Song of Songs, the maiden sees her life and ministry as His garden. The words of love from His lips have worked powerfully in her. Love has opened her eyes. Revelation is flowing. Understanding is developing. She belongs to Him. All of life is about Him, not just her.

The Bride longs for the King to come to His garden (her inner life and ministry) and taste the fruits of His grace. She really wants Jesus to come and enjoy what the Spirit has done within her. She waits for a visitation. . . .

"Let my Lover come into His garden and taste its choice fruits. . . . " She prays, "Come enjoy Yourself in me." Everything in this garden is grown by Him and for Him. Since she is His inheritance, she invites Him to enjoy it (Eph. 1:18). Her whole life has changed focus from what *she* gets out of it to what **He** gets out of her! The love song of Jesus is maturing the Bride. Can He feast His heart in you? Jesus awaits your invitation. . . .

Seven times Jesus said, **"My"** — she has truly become His very own. The ownership of her life and ministry has been transferred over to Him. **"My garden . . . My sister, My Bride . . . My honey . . . My wine. . . ."** Jesus now answers her prayer in 4:16, He has come to *His* garden to enjoy *His* inheritance. This is a wonderful time of nearness for her . . . she has changed.

She is now able to give her love more fully to Him. She understands that her identity is a lover of God. She is moving into advanced stages of dedication. For now, she is the garden of delight to the King.

The King Enjoys His Inheritance

"I have gathered My myrrh with My spice." The Lord comes to His church to gather from us what He has worked in us.[1] Jesus comes to draw from our hearts the expressions of love and adoration He deserves. He visits us to see if we have embraced His Cross (myrrh), and have experienced the graces of God in our walk with Him (spices). The King *will* come to His garden when there are fruits and spices to satisfy Him.

"I have eaten My honeycomb and My honey." Jesus comes to feast on the honeycomb of a mature church. His Bride has become nourishment for Him. She asked Him to come and eat; now He has done so. How the Lord is blessed by what the Spirit has done in His Bride! Delightful food is being served all over the world as Jesus feasts on our love.

"I have drunk My wine and My milk." Our Lord Jesus has quenched His thirst with the wine of our loving devotion. He celebrates all that grace has accomplished in our lives. She has given Him all He has desired. *Wine* is for celebration; *milk* is for strength. This is union and communion in the Holy Place. Our love feast with Jesus brings joy and encouragement to His heart!

Jesus invites His friends to come and eat from the maturity and grace upon the Bride. **"Eat, O friends . . . drink your fill, O lovers. . . . "** This is awesome. She has grown from one who neglected her inner life, angered by those who wounded her, consumed with selfishness — to a maturing Bride that can be offered to the nations as meat and drink! Jesus wants others to enjoy the fruitfulness of His maturing Bridal Partner. The Bride has become the Banquet Table for others.

Do you long to be food for the immature? This is what Jesus meant when He said to Peter: *"Feed my sheep,"* and to his disciples when He said, *"You give them something to eat"* (Luke 9:13). Jesus brings His friends into His garden to share the fruit of the Bride. Those who are beginning in the early stages of Holy Passion (Song of Songs 1:2) are invited in to feast on the maturity of the Church that loves Jesus wholeheartedly.[2] As we allow the Lord to cultivate His garden, to grow His fruit within us — He will take what is His and feed others with it. We then, become a true shepherd that feeds the flock. This is how we become shepherds for the immature to follow (1:8).

---

[1] He does this with His five fingered hand (Eph. 4:11, the 5-fold ministry).
[2] Note the parallel of Jacob in Gen.29:1-10. Jacob becomes a type of Christ who rolls the stone away from his well to water the sheep.

"Open to Me,
My sister, My darling . . .
My dove . . .
My flawless one."

Song of Songs 5:2
౭ఌ

The Splendor of the Bridegroom

Chapter 5:2-16
ಶ⧸ಣ

Spiritual maturity is taking up our cross, following Jesus, and becoming His loving disciples. Wisdom has a cross. Calvary Road is a path reserved for every true follower of the Lamb. When we embrace the cross, we begin to cherish the things that matter to Jesus. We become a radiant Bride . . . one that Jesus will share His life with. Be ready for a fresh vision of the Tree of Life, the cross of Jesus . . . come, eat of its fruit. . . .

The Lord Jesus loves to come to us in different forms, imparting new revelation of who He is. This time, He comes not as the Sweet Savior or the Leaping Prince, but as the Man of Sorrows. We cannot embrace a part of Jesus; we must receive all of Him. Every new season of our lives will bring a new understanding of Jesus, the Glorious Son of God. Now a new season has come . . . a season of testing. The love of her King has accomplished much. She has grown; she has been transformed . . . but there is still more of Jesus she must discover. After hearing His incredible statements of affirmation, after crying out for the north winds she falls asleep. Alone in her chamber she dreams of His approach. . . . **"I slept"** — This is also the rest of faith and confidence that all is well;

fleshly activity has ceased. She has committed to going to the mountain of myrrh and paying the price. **"But my heart was awake."** Obedience has made her awake to the things of God. She is not asleep in the compromise of Laodecia (Rev. 3), but remains awake to righteousness (I Thess. 5:6, Rom. 13:11). As she lies there in bed, the Lord Jesus draws near. Our King comes unannounced in the night seasons to speak His heart to us. . . .

"Listen! My Lover is knocking. . . . "[1] The Bride is now sensitive to the voice of the Bridegroom. He comes to her, knocking on the door of her heart. It is the voice of the Beloved that knocks on her heart's door. He longs to take her through a new door in the spirit (Rev. 3:8, 20). This new door, if opened, will lead to a new revelation of Jesus in her life. Outside the door, knocking, He calls her with these words, **"Open to ME."**

There is music in His voice . . . music that awakens her. Who would not open the door when Jesus draws near singing His song? How could we refuse entry to this One who has not one unkind or angry word? When He comes knocking on your door will you open the door and let Him in?

He calls her with four terms of endearment: **"My sister, My darling, My dove, My flawless one."**[2] Jesus is the ultimate Source of tenderness and compassion. His knock is good; there is nothing to fear when He calls us. As He looks into the eyes of the maiden, He can see that she is fully His . . . she is flawless. His words of encouragement wash over her . . . preparing her for the greatest challenge of her life. . . . She has cried for the north winds.

She is willing to embrace the cross. Now comes the ultimate test. . . .

"My head is drenched with dew, My hair with the dampness of the night." Who is this One coming in the middle of the night? Only a person who was outside all night would have the dew upon his hair. This is the Jesus of Gethsemane, the One who lay awake all night long praying for you and I (John 17, Ps. 22:2, Luke 22:44). He is the One who endured the dark night of the soul and now invites her to join Him in the fellowship of His sufferings (Isa. 53, Phil. 3:10). He is calling her to share His shame, rejection, and loneliness.

This revelation of Jesus is far different than any other she has seen thus far. Jesus stands outside knocking, wanting her to embrace the Cross as He did. We want the Jesus of the Banquet Table, we want the Jesus who leaps over mountains, but will we embrace the Jesus of Gethsemane? Can we not watch and pray with Him one hour?

Our Lord Jesus was a Man of Sorrows and was acquainted with grief. It is time for her to know His heart, to share His burdens. This was a call to enter into deeper fellowship with the Magnificent Intercessor. As Jesus struggled in prayer in the garden of Gethsemane, He sweat drops of blood as He faced His agony. Will He find her prepared for this test? The Crucified One must have crucified followers.

"I have taken off my robe, must I put it on again?" He had labored all night in prayer and agony while she slept on her bed in comfort. Her response to the knock shows she is satisfied with what she has experienced so far. Taking off her robe is the outward work of the cross (taking off her robe of righteousness), a picture of laying aside the old life . . . but has she truly tasted the cup of His death and sufferings? She has washed her feet by confessing her sins,[3] but has she inwardly given herself over to death to self and His resurrection life?[4] Her cry is simply, "Isn't it enough that I have an outward life of goodness?" He came to disturb her spiritual ease. She felt that she had experienced all there was to the cross . . . but there is more. . . .

God's plan for us is to reveal the Cross, deal with us regarding our deep need of Him, and unite us to His death and resurrection. For her to learn these deeper lessons, she must endure the "dark night of the soul," a season where Jesus withdraws from her with no explanation. Can she love Him even while she doesn't sense His presence?

He Touches the Door of Her Heart

"My Lover thrust His hand[5] through the latch-opening. . . . " He comes in grace to touch her. The heart is that everlasting gateway that swings open to the King (Ps. 24:7). **"My heart began to pound for Him."** The Vulgate, the first Latin translation of the Bible, reads, *"My soul melted when He spoke."* Just one touch from Him and our hearts melt with desire to know Him as He really is. Like the disciples on the road to Emmaus, our hearts burn within us to be close to this Lovely One. The King was trying to get into the room. This touch on the latch-opening of her soul caused her to arise and seek Him. She could not stay in bed when He was near. . . .

"I arose to open for my Lover" —She arises in full obedience to open the door to Him. Just as she said "yes" to the north winds, she says "yes" to the Jesus of Gethsemane. But He had gone. . . . As the maiden opened the door for Him liquid myrrh dripped from her hands. This speaks of her inward life impacted by the sufferings of her Savior.

The **"flowing myrrh"** points to an abundance of grace that helps us to *fully* embrace God's will. She is drenched with a desire to walk the way of the cross. The outstretched hand opening the door is a picture of her will in action to pursue the Lord. The myrrh on the lock was His calling card . . . the anointing of His sufferings still lingered with her.

"He was gone"

Every sincere believer will someday endure the tests that the Shulamite had to go through. We will not be made mature without the testing of our faith. Most of us do not have a theology that accepts hardships. We tend to interpret difficulty as either punishment from God or the direct activity of Satan. Often, it is simply God's way of training and bringing us to the place of maturity. There is no need to bind Satan every time life is rough, nor is it always a sign of God's displeasure. Those He loves, He disciplines. The departure of Jesus in this place in the story is *because* she is abandoned to Him, needing the gust of the north wind to blow on her garden to make the fruit sweeter. He has addressed her as one without flaw . . . His dove.

"My heart sank at His departure."[6] She was moved at the sound of His voice—"Open to Me." Her heart leaped up in obedience when He wanted in, but now, *"He was gone."* He hides His face from her, so quickly He is gone! It is time now in her journey to understand that God is a God who hides Himself (Ps. 74:11, Prov. 25:2, Isa. 45:15, Hos. 5:6, Luke 22:41).

Immediately she begins to drink of the cup of loneliness and rejection. This is not an attack of the devil; it is the sovereign purpose of God worked out in her life. This God-ordained test will move her into Christ-likeness. The Gethsemane Man is about to teach her of the Cross. There is a test from God that is totally unrelated to rebellion. Too often, we are like Job's friends that concluded that Job was being afflicted because he was in hidden sin. God will hide His face from the most devout to draw their hearts into pure pursuit, making them wholly His (Job 30:12-31).

During this "dark night of the soul," we can see what is in the deepest parts of our hearts and see our true motives. Jesus told Peter that his faith would be sifted like wheat. Will you be fervent and seek the Lord without the feeling of His presence? Do you pursue solely for your own spiritual pleasure, or will you pursue Him for His sake alone? Can you be faithful regardless of the circumstances of your life?

"I looked for Him but did not find Him." This is a test of major proportions. . . . He cannot be found and He will not answer her cry. Seeking and praying cannot shorten this test; she must experience it fully. She throws on her robe and runs barefoot into the streets looking for her Beloved. **"I called Him but He did not answer."** Has this ever happened to you? He will train us by hiding from us. The silence of a hiding God must do its work in our soul.

When the Lord withdraws the sense of His presence, we lose joy while worship becomes a struggle. We may feel helpless and useless. God seems silent;no amount of pleading brings Him out of hiding. These moments test us severely, but they bring forth fruit that will remain. As we refuse the devil's voice of accusation we are able to live under the truth: "His banner over me is love."

"The watchmen found me . . . they beat me"

As she runs through the streets shouting, she awakens the neighborhood . . . as only angry shouts respond to her cries. Then the watchmen of the city come to investigate. Persecution and rejection meet her as the watchmen encounter the confused maiden. The watchmen are those in spiritual authority. They are the governmental ministries in the Body of Christ. She has met the David-type watchmen in 3:3 who are there to help her find a place of deeper intimacy with Jesus. Now the Saul-type watchmen that are motivated by jealousy and fear abuse her.

The jealous watchmen find her, they beat her, bruising her.[7] Their jealousy causes them to discredit those who are in passionate pursuit of Jesus. They find others and begin to wound them with accusations and blame. God has given them a mandate to protect, but instead they use authority in a heavy-handed way to hurt the weak, stumbling . . . those struggling in the dark night of their souls. They did not recognize the Shulamite as the Bride of the King.

This is a severe test indeed, to be persecuted by those who should protect. Rising up against her they take away her cloak (ministry covering) and bruise her cruelly. When those placed "over us" unjustly persecute us, it brings a wounding that is hard to describe. Mistreatment from friends and leaders is a test that few will escape. Even Jesus was wounded in the house of His friends (Ps. 55:12-21).

What is her response to this twofold test of maturity? She has faced the dark night of her soul. Jesus, the Bridegroom, has left her. . . . Only the smell of myrrh dripping from her fingers reminds her that it was more than a dream. Looking for her Lover only left her wounded and bleeding from the mistreatment of leaders. God's presence was withdrawn, and now the Body has turned against her. Her covering is removed and she is cast out, losing her place of ministry (temporarily) in the Body of Christ. She cried out for the north winds and they have now come to perfect her faith. He answered her prayer for the north winds because He wanted to expose the unperceived areas of weakness in her heart.

Will you embrace Gethsemane? When everything is gone can you still serve Jesus with fervent love? Will you continue to love the Body when they treat you badly? With all the feelings of pain, hurt, and dishonor, she responds . . . **"O daughters of Jerusalem . . . if you find my Lover, what will you tell Him? Tell Him I am faint with love."** She loves Him no matter what. She is in it for Him. "It is you Lord that is my passion. No matter what they do to me. No matter if I can feel You or not. I am love-sick for You." She is not offended at Him for what happened, she is love-sick!

The sorrowing bride wandering in the dark turns to the daughters of Jerusalem, "Tell my Lover that I can't stand it anymore. I love Him more than I can tell, for I am overcome with love! Tell Him I'm not mad. Tell Him I'm not offended at what others did. Tell Him I am faint with love!" The Shulamite has passed the ultimate test . . . she loves Him still.

Her friends can't understand how she could still love Him so. They can see the strength of her love, but in their amazement they ask, **"How is your Beloved better than others?"** We do not realize how loudly our faith speaks when we persevere in a time of testing. The immature are strengthened to know our Beloved when they see us faithful in the fires of testing. Just asking this question shows their lack of perception. They cannot understand such devotion during testing. But to her, He has no rival.

The maidens address the Shulamite as **"most beautiful of women."** They show a deep respect for this one that has remained loyal, in love with the King. They are able to see His beauty starting to shine upon her; her godliness, her devotion, and purity point them to Him.

The essence of their question is really, "How can you be so in love with One who treats you like this? Tell us the secret; what is it about your Beloved?" Silence falls on the friends, waiting to see if she will answer.

The Bride gives them one of the clearest, most glorious descriptions of Jesus Christ found in the Bible. With trembling lips she begins to tell them about her Husband. . . . She has fallen in love with One who has blinded her to all others.

The Splendor of the Bridegroom

The love-sick Bride can never be turned away from the Beauty of Jesus. Everything about Him is beyond description. He is altogether lovely. There is none other like Him. The twofold test of Jesus hiding from her and the Body wounding her has brought her to a new revelation of the splendor of her Bridegroom.

We are about to gaze upon the unveiled glory of the Son of God. The awakened Bride gives us a poetic listing of the virtues of Jesus. Once you have seen Him you cannot draw back from pursuing His presence. Instead of being offended that He had left her for a season, she sets her heart on His beauty and excellence.

You and I must fill our hearts with the revelation of Jesus in our time of testing. Every aspect of His personality has the power to revive and restore your soul when you are under pressure. This is why the Scriptures teach us to *"fix our eyes on Jesus"*[8] when we are tested or burdened. His life is the one Life that always pleases the Father. To abide in Him means to draw from these virtues the strength that our weak hearts need.

"My Lover is radiant and ruddy." No matter what happens, He is still her Lover. She has kept the fires burning even during the dark night of the soul. There are times it is quite difficult to call Him our Lover when our heart is wounded. She is not offended over how He treated her (Matt. 11:6). It is important to let down our guard to Him when we do not understand what He is doing in our circumstances. When we cannot see His face we can trust His heart. Call Him your Lover and His brightness will turn the shadows to daybreak. He is radiant.

The word radiant means "dazzling, sunny, or bright." Even in a time of difficulty and pain, Jesus shines brightly in our night. He is absolutely brilliant in His radiance and stunning in His splendor.

What glorious colors surround His throne, for He dwells in abundance of light (I Tim. 6:16)! In appearance, He is compared to the sardius and jasper stones (Rev. 4:2). Sardius is a deep red stone, while jasper is a transparent green. This radiance speaks of His Divine Nature; God poured into human flesh!

The word ruddy means red or "rosy cheeks." The **"ruddy"** nature of Jesus is His human one. Our Lord Jesus is both Divine & Human! He is **"outstanding among ten thousand."** This speaks of the supremacy and uniqueness of Jesus; there is just no equal to Him (Col. 1:18)! It is not hard to see how wonderful He is . . . for He stands out in a crowd. He is the Radiant, Shimmering One who is spotless and pure. Jesus is incomparably more beautiful and more noble, than ten thousand great men combined. . . . He stands above them all! (Ps. 45:2, 84:11, Hab. 3:4, Matt. 17:2, Rev. 1:12-18, Dan. 7:9). The number "ten thousand" is the number of infinity. Jesus Christ stands infinitely above all the sons of men. He is the lovely and delightful Prince of Heaven!

What follows is a magnificent tenfold description of the Bridegroom. She is now gazing at Him and worshipping Him in the beauty of holiness. She will use the metaphors of the physical body to convey the virtues and glory of the Man Christ Jesus. This is the Ancient of Days, the Creator of heaven and earth. Here are some features about the life and leadership of our King:

1. Sovereign Leadership — *"His head is purest gold"*
　　Jesus' head of pure gold points us to the Divine quality of His leadership over us (Dan. 2:32-38,

Eph. 1:20-21, Col. 2:10). The highest degree of excellence is found in the leadership traits of our Lord Jesus. There is no Head like Him. There is no mixture of impurity with His wisdom. He leads His flock with compassion and wisdom, strength and mercy.

Jesus is the wisdom of God (I Cor. 1:30). His wisdom is like the finest gold because He has come from the Holiest of Holies; on His head are many crowns of gold (Rev. 19:12). His ruling grace combines all the attributes of God in lovely perfection. Blessed are those who have Jesus as their King. In the all-glorious head of gold, the maiden sees the qualities of the Headship of Jesus over everything.

2. <u>Holy Dedication</u> — *"His hair is wavy . . . black as a raven"*

Jesus was wholly devoted to God. The Nazarite vow forbid one to cut his hair; long hair then becomes a sign of devotion to God. The thick, black, wavy hair was a sign of His youthfulness, His zeal and vigor (in contrast to balding or gray hair). Jesus is forever young, energetic and zealous in His Holy devotion to God and men. He is the same yesterday, today, and forever (Heb. 13:8). His priestly ministry flows from the power of an endless life (Heb. 7:16).

3. <u>Loving Insight</u> — *"His eyes . . . doves by the water streams"*

Jesus' eyes speak of His perception, His infinite knowledge, His wisdom and understanding. His eyes like doves tell us that He has singleness of vision and can look upon us with purity. Even when He sees what is wrong with us, His dove's eyes cover us in love. Like doves by the water streams, His eyes view us through the cleanliness of divine insight. His discernment of us is untainted by anger or rejection. He has Holy Spirit anointed vision that is washed in love. His All-Seeing eyes detect what is yet to be perfected and brought to maturity.

"Washed in milk" speaks again of the purity of His gaze. A judge may know all the facts about an event, but if his heart is unclean he will not properly interpret it. Jesus' eyes are clean, washed in milk to nourish weak faith and to set in order mixed motives. He can see the sincerity of our hearts, even when our deeds are immature. He is always watching over us and calling us beautiful. He sees every private act of righteousness, every time we do not give up under pressure. He takes note of our positive response to misunderstanding or persecution. He sees the money given to His kingdom. He sees it when you put Him first.

When we have a revelation of His eyes like doves, we don't have to always set the record straight, or insist that others understand us. We won't feel the compulsion to tell our glory stories or exaggerate what God has helped us to accomplish. Knowing that we are in His gaze day after day is enough! **"Mounted like jewels"**—no deformity, no twisted vision. His eyes are sparkling like rare gemstones. There is such beauty in everything about Jesus. The way that He views us with sparkling eyes melts our hearts.

4. Exquisite Emotions—*"His cheeks are like beds of spice ... "*
His countenance is always gracious. The emotions of Jesus are like a garden filled with delightful fragrances. His cheeks are windows into His emotional makeup. Everything about Jesus is extraordinary. His emotions are diverse and refreshing. The Hebrew

word for "cheeks" is taken from a root word that means *soft*—Jesus is tender of heart. From His heart flowed the kindest of words ever spoken (John 8:11-12). He always gives a soft answer that turns away wrath (Prov. 15:1). "Beds of spice" is *bosem*, which means *creating desire*. The life and personality of Jesus awakens the desire within us to know Him.

5. <u>Life-giving Words</u> — *"His lips are like lilies . . . "*

His lips were truthful lips (Prov. 12:19). No man has ever spoken like He did (Isa. 50:4). His lips were anointed with grace (Ps. 45:2, Luke 4:22, John 7:46). His life was full of prayer and praise. The words from His lips are always life-giving and encouraging. His words are Spirit and Life, every word pure as a lily (John 6:63). The affirming words of Jesus are tender and sweet as a lily. His lips kissed heaven in worship and kissed children in compassion. But myrrh was the secret of His anointing.

The myrrh on the speech of Jesus brings people into the revelation of the Cross. His words will always exhort us to embrace the Cross and die to self. When His Word truly comes to us, it is sharper than any two-edged sword, piercing through our excuses and touches us deeper than any other thing. The lily gives a sweet smell while the myrrh has a sense of suffering attached. Both sweetness and boldness can be found on the lips of our King.

6. <u>Perfect Power</u> — *"His arms are rods of gold. . . . "*

The arm of the Lord is His power demonstrated in human affairs. His hands are mighty and effective in accomplishing exactly what is in His heart. This power is like rods of gold. The golden rods of power are holy displays of omnipotence. Jesus Christ is the Rod of

God, the Rod of Moses, Aaron's Rod that budded in the Holy Place, Isaiah's Branch of the Lord, and the Father's Scepter of Righteousness. His holy arms are **"rods of gold."** Everything God's arm accomplishes is pure and golden, powerful and glorious.

"Set with chrysolite." This is the beryl, a jewel that shines like a diamond. All the works of Jesus are golden, skillfully set like a beautiful jewel. His wise skill in all that He does will shine throughout eternity. His deeds display power, but with kindness and goodness. Do you see God's power at work in you like a rod of gold? You must discern the beauty in every activity of Jesus in your heart (Rev. 15:4). This ability to see His works as lovely is a sign of maturity. Even His puzzling works are like rods of gold, set with chrysolite.

7. <u>Tender Compassion</u> — *"His body . . . like polished ivory"*

Other translations of this are "his belly" or "his yearning heart." The use of this particular Hebrew word conveys the meaning of tender compassion, a yearning heart (Isa. 63:15, Jer. 31:20). There is no one who enjoys weak people like Jesus. He is the most compassionate, tender One to the failing, struggling believer. Out of His innermost being flows rivers of God's love for thirsty hearts. . . .

"Like polished ivory" — Clean and bright, this is how He deals with us. His mercy "polishes" our heart. . . . Jesus is uniquely understanding of the weaknesses of others. Most great people are impatient with the weaknesses of those under them — yet our King has the rarest of mercies toward all (Ex. 34:6).

"Decorated with sapphires." The sapphire stone is listed as one of the gems attached to Aaron's breastplate and is one of the foundation stones of the New

Jerusalem (Rev. 21:19). On the sapphire stone the name of Simeon was scratched. Simeon means, "He who hears." On the innermost being of Jesus is marked, "He who hears." How we rejoice in this One who always hears the Father!

The Throne of God is a "sapphire throne" (Ezek. 1:26). In Isaiah 54:11, the loving Bridegroom speaks of the Bride (City) as having foundation stones of "sapphires." To mount a sapphire stone into ivory would take time, skill, and creativity. This is how exquisite the compassion of our Lord is towards us. God's affections are rare, pure, creative, and tender. His love polishes us until we look like sapphires.

8. <u>Ways of Wisdom</u> — *"His legs are pillars marble. . . . "*

Jesus walks in a wisdom beyond measure. His legs (His ways) are always executed with strength and dignity. Nothing can stop Him when He is determined to act; His legs are pillars of marble! He does not fail to accomplish what He desires; He does not waiver under pressure. The dependable ways of our King are like marble rock pillars. Even in her testing the bride has a pillar to hold her up.

"Set on bases of pure gold." These are the Divine foundations upon which righteousness rests. Whatever our Lord does, it is based on purity, holiness and truth (Rev. 15:3, Ps. 25:10). His character is golden from head to toe! The soldiers on Golgotha's hill did not break His legs (John 19:33). The Rock of Ages stands!

9. <u>His Excellency</u> — *"His appearance is like Lebanon"*

When you gaze at the appearance of our Lover-Friend, it is truly awe inspiring. It is like looking at a mountain range. Every feature of His countenance, every facet of His wisdom and ways are colorful and rewarding. Jesus, You are excellent in every aspect of your appearance. I love everything about You, Jesus! Beauty streams into our lives when we keep looking unto Him. His countenance imparts light and joy to our spirits. Just looking at Him deposits something virtuous into our lives. Looking at His face is like looking over Lebanon—a symbol of strength and stately beauty.

"Choice as its cedars." The tall, strong cedar trees full of fragrance.... The cedars of Lebanon were called the "king of trees." All of this is a glorious picture of who Jesus has become to the Bride lost in love. He is the Evergreen Tree with eternal life (Heb: 13:8). The glory of God is seen in the face of Jesus Christ (II Cor. 4:6). Looking at Jesus is the theme and object of our devotion....

10. <u>Intimacy With Him</u>—*"His mouth is sweetness itself"*

Jesus can give us a sacred intimacy with Himself that is like sweetness to the soul. O, the sweetness of Jesus! He is all delight to my soul. Every pleasure, every source of entertainment and temporary joy— they all fade in comparison to one "kiss" of sacred intimacy. This is the "sweetest," most pleasing experience known to the human spirit. It transforms us over time. It releases an affirmation that lets us soar when times are rough. To know Him is to love Him. To love Him is to be loved by Him. To be loved by Him is heaven. Heaven is the eternal "kiss" of Jesus Christ!

He Is Altogether Lovely

How could we comprehend the intoxicating beauty of our Lord? His love is out of sight; His mercy is above the heavens; His holiness makes mountains melt; His majesty causes seraphim to cover their faces. His affection breaks our heart. Every beautiful melody, every radiant sunrise, every work of art and beauty points us to Him. Altogether lovely is our Prince and King. Have you ever found anything that is not loveable about Jesus?

Every aspect of Jesus is radiant and lovely when taken together. Look on Him from whatever position you wish and He is altogether desirable. There is nothing disagreeable or distracting when you gaze upon Him. Every desire of a Bride can be found in Him. With delight He satisfies our every longing for a life partner. Nothing else can even be compared to Him. . . . Remember, she says all of this without Him near. He has left her for a season, yet her praise and joy is in Him.

The Hebrew reads, "He is all *desires!*" This can also be translated *"admirable, graceful, delectable, most pleasant or earnestly desirable."* The original word is plural in number. . . . Jesus is all *desires*. He is every desire fulfilled. Jesus is all your dreams come true. He is the essence of every delight and pleasure. As every river flows to the ocean and is gathered as one, so Christ becomes to the believer's soul the ocean of true desires. Jesus is bread to the hungry, water to the thirsty, a garment to the naked and healing for the wounded. Whatever your soul could desire, Jesus is that and more!

Jesus is altogether lovely simply because of who He is. He is Deity dwelling in the flesh—the wonderful and perfect union of God and man. Overflowing with the graces of the Spirit, Jesus becomes the Most Lovely of all the sons of men. Jesus is altogether lovely as the Light to the world, as the Way to the Father and as the Truth that sets men free. He is the Great Prophet to bring us back to God, the Great High Priest to keep us near the heart of our Father and He is the Great King who leads and governs His House with grace and glory.

There is no other friend so open-hearted as Jesus to you and I. He shares His secrets with us and sympathizes with us in all our failures and weaknesses. He is altogether kind as He feels our sorrows and carries our burdens. He is the Lovely Lamb that took away all our sins. . . . Isn't He wonderful!

The question still asked is this: "Who do you say that I am?"[9] He is so much more than what we have thought, so much more than what we've been told, so much more than our understanding is able to contain. Altogether lovely, without flaw. His garment of righteousness is without seam. All of His perfections flow into unity and wholeness. All the languages of men and angels combined cannot describe him! Awesome, yet playful. Affectionate, yet terrifying. Dancing with us, yet breaking our hearts. Most tender, yet transcendent. When you have seen Him in His splendor you could never turn away from Him.

"This is my Lover,[10] this is my Friend!" Can you see why the Bride could not be offended by the training course she was enduring? The glory of the Bridegroom was infinitely greater than the pain of her process of growth. She calls Him "my Lover . . . my Friend." He is not only the Sovereign One whose head is finest gold, He is also One who embraces us me as true friends. What a Savior!

Listen as the maturing Bride speaks of Him with great passion and feeling. . . .

"This is my Lover, this is my Friend." He is both dearly beloved and Faithful Friend. There is no other friend like Jesus. *Never* will He disappoint you or walk away when you fail. He is reliable and true. There has never been a husband like He. She has endured the dark night of the soul without a sense of His nearness. How strong is her love for Him!

---

[1] This is *the* Old Testament commentary of Rev. 3:20. Jesus is the Heavenly Bridegroom who knocks on the door of the Laodicean church.

[2] Five times in this verse He uses the terms, "Me" and "My."

[3] To wash feet is a picture of our outward cleansing through confession and repentance of known sin (John 13).

[4] Bare feet signify a slave before a master.

[5] The hand that reached out to her was a nail-pierced hand.

[6] Or, "My heart went out to Him when He spoke."

[7] Note: Even the immature "Davids" who lack wisdom and tenderness to the sheep are also capable of wounding others.

[8] Hebrews 12:2

[9] See Matthew 16:15.

[10] From II Samueul 2:25 we learn that King David named his son Solomon with another name . . . Jedidiah. Both the names of David and Jedidiah are from the same Hebrew root words which means "beloved." Jesus Christ is our Beloved.

The King Overwhelmed

Chapter 6:1-13
ଔ୦ଓଷ

$\mathcal{T}$he Love of Jesus is truly beyond description. It takes the Song of all Songs to even begin to impart it to the hearts of fallen men. This story is the greatest love story of all eternity. Some day, Jesus will step out of heaven and rip the sky open to take this Bride unto Himself. All of Hollywood's genius could not put together a better ballad than this glorious Song.

The Daughters of Jerusalem listened as the maiden extolled the virtues of her Bridegroom. They were spellbound to hear of One so altogether lovely. Now they too want to search for Him. In time, they will become the Shulamite of Chapter 1:2, and the Song will be sung again over them. In Chapter 5:9 they asked, "*Who* is He?" After hearing the Bride's glorious description of the Bridegroom they now question her: "*Where* is He?"

When others see His beauty, they too will be gripped by holy passion. The goal of all ministry must be to express the splendor of Christ Jesus. The anointed answer of the Shulamite convinced the daughters of Jerusalem that they too must follow after Him. They have to know, *where can you find Him?*

"Where has your Love gone, most beautiful of women?" Others view her as a godly example of the One she follows. The splendor of Jesus has made her beautiful to others. They are using the same phrase that Jesus used to describe her in 1:8. They see her the same way Jesus sees her. Her longing for Jesus above all others has made her life attractive and beautiful. **"Which way did your Lover turn?"** They repeat the question, revealing their earnest longing to know Him the way the Bride knows Him.

He is still only *her* Lover, not yet *their* Lover. **"That we may look for Him with you."** They are convicted of their distance from Him; they must join in pursuit of this King. They want to look for Him alongside of her. We really only find Jesus as we are in fellowship with others rather than in isolation. With a humble and teachable heart, they join together in seeking Him. They are about to become the longing maiden of 1:2 and begin their journey. . . .

He Is Within His Garden

"My Lover has gone down to His garden. . . . " As she ponders their question it dawns on her . . . "I know where He has gone. . . . I know where His garden is. . . . I am His garden. . . . He is within me!" The Garden of the Lord is His church. Jesus is found among His people. This is the lesson repeated throughout the Song of Songs (and throughout the Bible).

We seem to forget in times of testing and spiritual thirst that Jesus is with His people. He loves to hang out with those who love Him. He does not wait until we are perfect before He dwells within us. He waits until we look for Him. He will be with us until the end of the age

(Matt. 28:20) and will love us all the way unto the end (John 13:1).

Beloved, you will find your Friend in His garden, the Church. This is the same answer He gave to the Shulamite in 1:8; *get involved with Body life. Follow the tracks of those who follow Me.* Your Lover is a Gardener who is always involved in making you fruitful and beautiful.

Too many Christians today are seeking an "out-of-Body" experience; that is, they believe they can find the Lord somewhere other than among His people. But the Lord of Glory will always be found with His people. The new experience Jesus wants you to have, you will have in relationship to His Body. We cannot truly find Him until we have found Him in the context of a corporate Life in His Church.

"To the beds of spices" — What different expressions of life can be found in His garden! None of us are the same. We are all like various spices that bring delight to Him when combined. He takes great pleasure in the diversity of His garden — like spice beds of varying flavors. The Lord wants us to value those who are different spices (different streams) in His garden. We can be glad that not all churches are like ours. Not all believers are like *us.*

There is spice in the church for Jesus. The saints are His special spice beds. The One who created love in us, will be delighted in what He sees. He comes to feed His heart on the variety of our expressions of love. Jesus loves His whole church, but He will manifest Himself differently to each one with varying levels of intensity.

"To browse in the gardens and to gather lilies . . . " This speaks of the deep pleasures that come to Jesus from partaking of the love of His Bride. He feeds His heart on the purity of our devotion to Him. He will go from garden to garden, lampstand to lampstand, to browse and gather lilies to Himself (Rev. 1:13, 20). The King enjoys each part of the Corporate Bride.

"Lilies" are the believers who are sincerely devoted to purity, innocence, and Bridal-loyalty to Jesus. To **"gather lilies"** is to unite the Bride as One to be only His (Matt. 23:37). When Jesus comes to us, He longs to see us united in the same love for each other as we have for Him. Our Savior will also come to gather the lost and make them "lilies" in His garden.

Fully His

"I am my Lover's, and my Lover is mine." This is one of the great statements made by the Bride in this narrative. She has heard Him call her His "garden," now she gives herself fully to Him. With new revelation, she is committed to His purpose and His pleasure. Up to now, she has primarily been seeking Him for *her* pleasure. Maturity has come. The focus of her life has now turned from self to the person of Jesus. Her whole life is now His as she is under His leadership.

To be His Bride is to understand that our existence on earth is for Him. We are not to spend life on self, but being poured out to Him. Her one desire is to be His inheritance. No one else has any claims on her. She is His and His alone, shared by none other. . . . She is His lily.

Her story is our story . . . a transition from a self-centered life to a life that is only His. All of us begin our journey into the heart of Jesus with the desire to please ourselves. Our own enjoyment of Jesus is the focus, not *His enjoyment of us*. We talk about what Jesus has done for *us* and what He is to *us*. This is the wonderful joy of knowing Him—and it is legitimate pleasure! But in time, we must mature in love — acknowledging His rights to enjoy us. We are Jesus' inheritance. He died to have us!

The thirst of His heart is to commune with His Bride and become life itself to each one of us. We exist for Him (Rev. 14:4-5)! Blessed are those who unconditionally serve God with no thought of themselves . . . they are like lilies in His garden.

Jesus Gazes Upon The Bride

As the maiden speaks with the daughters of Jerusalem, the Lord Jesus suddenly breaks His silence. **"You are beautiful, My darling."** He praises His Bride, communicating His deepest feelings toward her. Remember . . . He had withdrawn from her (5:2), which brought her out into the dark night to find Him. Jesus had been testing her heart. Now that He has heard her description of Him, and her extravagant worship (5:10-16), the King praises her using three wonderful metaphors: **"beautiful as Tirzah, lovely as Jerusalem, and majestic as troops with banners."**

Tirzah and Jerusalem were the two main cities of Israel. Tirzah, the northern capitol, and Jerusalem, the southern capital. The name "Tirzah" actually means, *beautiful* or *pleasing*. It was named Tirzah because of its remarkable natural beauty. Jesus is reaffirming His love for her during the season He was distant from her. Using terms of endearment, He compares her heart of loving affection to the natural beauty of the city of Tirzah. Nine times in the Song of Songs the Bridegroom praises her beauty (1:15 twice, 2:10, 2:13, 4:1 twice, 4:7, 6:4, 7:7). Never has there been a king like this One. . . . never has there been a king who loves his people like this One.

Jerusalem was the capital city and the joy of the whole earth. God's very presence dwelt over the Holy of Holies in the Temple of Jerusalem. The loyal love of the Bride is compared to the holy city of Jerusalem, possessing the glory of God. Just as Jerusalem was the center of worship, so her inner beauty is seen by her worship during times of severe testing. Just as Jerusalem is the dwelling place of God, so He can say of her: "How lovely is your dwelling place" (Ps. 84:1)! The real loveliness of her spirit in the fruit of her trials—she has endured with persevering love. This beauty is what He Himself has perfected in her. His love for us makes us beautiful. Beloved, you are the lovely dwelling place of God.

The Scriptures speak of God's people as a city. We are like a city set on a hill (Matt. 5:13). Abraham looked for this city, whose builder and architect was God. Abraham looked for two things . . . *a city* raised up by God and *a bride* for His Son. John the Apostle found them both in the glorified church! When the Bride is adorned for her Husband, she will come down from heaven as a city (Rev. 21). The New Jerusalem is not merely a place, but a people. The Bridal Community that God will establish on the earth someday will be those who are adorned with His beauty. Jesus will not give His Bride a diamond ring . . . He will give her a diamond city!

Not only is the victorious Bride like a radiant city, but she will appear as a troop waving banners. This speaks of a victorious army. Only armies that were victorious would come back to the city waving their banners in majestic procession. A defeated army lost its banners to their conquerors. Troops with banners were those who walked in great victory maintaining order and rank. She had learned the lessons of spiritual authority and understood that she was victorious as she followed the King.

Striking beauty and majestic power now characterize the Bride. She is ready to demolish the enemy. She is a Bride with combat boots! Walking under His authority is the key to spiritual victory over dark powers. She has walked through her season of testing with victory. She has remained loyal to Him no matter what. Jesus calls His Bride awesome, like a mighty army waving banners of victory! The banner of love (2:4) becomes her banner of victory in times of affliction.

Jesus Overwhelmed

"Turn your eyes from Me, they overwhelm Me!" How can it be that Jesus sees His Bride with such compassion! We are lovely in His sight. When we pursue Him in the midst of our pain with loyal love, His heart is moved beyond description. He tells the worshipping Bride to stop gazing at Him; "I can't take it anymore." Beloved, when your eyes of faith are fixed on Him do you know what that does to Jesus? Your look of love overwhelms His heart! Your eyes of faith prevail over the Son of God!

The Shulamite has been sifted like wheat, tested over and over . . . and all this time she didn't even have a clue that her devotion was irresistibly beautiful to the King. So He uses poetic language asking her to turn away her gaze. Jesus could not withstand her ceaseless adoration anymore than one man could withstand an army coming against him. This is the great power of your love.

You truly have hold of the heart of your Lover-Friend when you worship with endless praise. . . . Imagine . . . your flashing eyes of fiery love overwhelm the mighty Son of God, the Prince of Glory! Your beautiful devotion overcomes His heart. The Eternal Bridegroom declares Himself defeated by the Bride. She has defeated Him with dove's eyes. She is still not perfect yet, and neither are you. She has yet to come out of her wilderness leaning on the Beloved, yet she has the capacity to ravish the heart of God! One of the great revelations of the Song of Songs is that even weak and incomplete believers overwhelm the heart of God as they turn to Him!

Jesus made the entire universe . . . The stars, the Milky Way, the constellations, the sky, fields and mountain peaks, yet none of creation's beauty overwhelms Him like you do! This Eternal King will one day lift up a rod of iron over the nations and use it to crush them to pieces. All of Satan's fury will come against the Coming King in that day of His splendor.

Even while no one can conquer or overcome Him . . . your glance of love leaves Him undone! Can you see what your enduring faithfulness to Jesus does to Him? Our love for Him in the midst of testing is more precious to the Bridegroom than we can take in. This Ultimate Warrior is so easily conquered by the devotion of His wife! Your eyes of passion are stronger than the Lord Jesus Christ!

In Exodus we read that God decided to destroy Israel for its idolatry of the golden calf. Moses' prayer defeated the plan of God. He made God change His mind. Every passionate, love-filled worshipper has power to move the heart of the King. The charm of your eyes is unbearable to the Bridegroom.

What Moses claimed through prayer can be your victory with merely one loving look . . . one glance of your eyes. This is why Christians are called more than conquerors; they are conquerors of the One who overcomes all!

He Describes Her Mature Dedication

"Your hair . . . your teeth . . . your temples . . . " She has grown from an immature maiden, who didn't have a clue as to what the King had prepared for her, to a strong devoted Bride. The repeated mention of hair, teeth, and temples reveals His unchanging love and her unwavering devotion to God. This is true love, face to Face—Her devotion and dedication, her maturity to digest and engraft the Word into her life, her emotions that are fully yielded to God and guarded (veiled) towards others.

Every feature of the Shulamite speaks of her growth in God. Hearing His words, gazing upon Him, and spending time in His presence has been the secret to her maturity. There is something so powerful, so alluring about our Jesus. Just being in His presence will radically change us deeply and forever. Think about this again: Jesus sees beauty in you. When he could point out our failures, our incomplete obedience, our immaturity, and weakness, He points to our virtues. This is our Bridegroom!

"Sixty queens[1] there may be, and eighty concubines, and virgins beyond number; but My dove, My perfect one is unique." These numbers sixty, eighty, and **"without number"** all represent the varying degrees of glory in the courts of God. Jesus proclaims that no one compares to the passionate Bride. Even the glorious ones in His courts cannot compete with her. The angelic host who does His bidding, no one is as preeminent as her.[2]

In the book of Esther, there were many in the harem of the king, but the queen was distinguished above all others. Concubines are those who dwell with the king but do not have the full legal rights of a queen. The full intimacy and authority before this King is reserved for only one, the Shulamite! There may be many in the King's courts, but she alone is His dove, His perfect one, unique above all others. The love of Jesus is so powerful that He can look at each one who pursues Him and call them unique.

"My dove, my perfect one, is unique. . . . " *You* are God's favorite one! Not only are you His favorite, you are called His **"perfect one!"** Can you imagine the Son of God looking at you with your failures, calling you His perfect one? Love has made you lovely. Redemption has given us the robe of righteousness. You are perfected for all time through the blood of Christ (Heb. 10:14). The perfection of the Shulamite is in her undefiled love. She is His magnificent obsession! He wants no other.

"The maidens saw her and called her blessed." All the immature believers marvel at the grace and dignity of the Bride. The grace upon her is attractive, bringing the praise of many. This is how the Bride will one day be seen. Spiritual maturity will be seen as glorious, not a legalistic denial or fanaticism. As the saints and angels marvel at God's wisdom manifest in the church, all jealousy will be removed.

"Like the dawn . . .fair . . . bright . . . majestic" The virgins, queens and concubines give their fourfold description of her in total amazement. **"Who is this . . . ?"** they ask. This is what the nations will acknowledge as they gaze upon the end time Bride of Christ (Isa. 61:9). It is a testimony of light and glory upon those who have been in deep spiritual communion with the Lord in His Holy Place. This is the Holy Spirit pointing to the uncommon beauty of the Bride, comparing her to the celestial objects. No longer a ragged goat-keeper, she is a radiant Bride!

1. **"Who is this that appears like the dawn?"** The morning light of personal victory is rising upon the church. In Chapter 2 she was looking *for* the morning, now she is looking *like* the morning! The dawn signals a new beginning, a new start in the things of God. With fresh mercy the church reaches out to the new day of His

appearing (Ps. 130:1-3, Lam. 3:22-23). She shines forth and appears like the dawn. . . . This is a picture of end time glory rising upon us! Just as a sunrise begins slowly, brightening the eastern sky, so the spiritual growth of each passionate follower of Jesus occurs gradually (Prov. 4:18). She had proclaimed, "Until the day breaks and the shadows flee," now it is happening! The shadows of compromise are leaving her as a new day of voluntary love begins.

2. **"Fair as the moon . . . "** or as "beautiful as the full moon (NAS)." There's a full moon rising! The church is seen in Scripture as the moon, reflecting the light of the Son. Ordained by God to give light to the world (Gen. 1:14-19), the church also reflects the light of Christ for a darkened planet (Phil. 2:15). All of our beauty comes from Jesus Christ. As a reflection of our Bridegroom, the church shines through the night season of His absence. Although marred by the craters of our sin, we shine, enduring the attack of Satan; ruling during the night seasons. The "faithful" witness of the full harvest moon speaks of our power to evangelize (Ps. 89:37, Matt. 5:16). Twelve times a year the moon gives forth her testimony; twelve is the number of Divine Government!

3. **"Bright as the sun . . . "** The increasing greatness of His glory is shining upon her. First the dim rays of sunrise appear, then the beauty of a full harvest moon . . . now she shines as clear as the sun! From glory to glory God will take us, until we carry the image of Jesus. God loves the Son so much that He will fill heaven with people just like Him!

Think about it. . . . We will someday be as *"bright as the sun!"* Deborah the prophetess/judge spoke of a day when those who love the Lord would shine like the sun "when it rises in its strength" (Judges 5:31). Jesus also spoke of a day when the "righteous will shine like the sun in the kingdom of their Father" (Matt. 13:43). Jesus is the "sun" of the celestial city (Rev. 21:23). The "sun of righteousness" will be the light of that city. Only the church is described with the same metaphor as the Lord Jesus (Rev. 12:1). As queen of the night and day, and queen of the new heavens and new earth, the Bride will carry His glory throughout eternity. She has now become a mirror that reflects the beauty of the Lord.

4. **"Majestic as the stars in procession."** The militant church is about to arise, awesome as an army with banners! The majestic army will experience total victory over every dark foe. As she triumphs over all sin, she becomes God's "war club" (Jer. 50:20). The stars are the armies of heaven who triumph over Satan and terrify the powers of darkness. His lovely Bride is like an army spreading out in the heavens with banners of praise.

How glorious is the love of God! What a holy injustice, to take former rebels and enthrone them on high. The Lord delights in giving His church His glory. What looks first like a sunrise on the horizon will one day light up the eternal city. . . . This is the advancing church.

His Cherished Companion

"I went down . . . to look at the new growth . . . " The Bride is now beginning to see her destiny. She has said "Yes" to full obedience, whatever the cost, even enduring the north winds of adversity. The Lord has shown her the unperceived fault lines beneath the surface of her life. As the cherished companion of Christ, she has received the fourfold testimony of the Lord (6:10). Now she is ready to turn toward the Body of Christ and be a blessing. A mature love for the church has grown within the maiden.

In the past, persecution and the immaturity of others have wounded her—but now she has changed. Philippians 2:3-4 is becoming a reality to her, she is ready to live for others. . . . *"Each of you should look not only to your own interests, but also to the interests of others."*

The **"grove of nut trees"** is quite a humorous description of the church, isn't it? We always knew there were "nuts" in the church! She humbles herself to *"go down"* and look at the "new growth" of other ministries. She goes down to the valley not only to look but to intercede for others. These ministries are compared to walnut trees. Just like a walnut, many of us have hard shells that must fall to the ground and die, before the fruit will appear (John 12:24). The walnut was once used for both soap and for food, cleansing and nourishment for others. Providing shade, these trees would someday become a source of refreshing to many.

The maiden comes humbly, willingly, to affirm and intercede for the growing ministries in the Body of Christ. Her self-consumed attitude is being replaced with true servanthood in the church.

Notice where the new growth is found . . . **"in the valley."** The low places of life are really the places of great fertility, as the fruit of Christ-likeness is brought forth out of our valleys. Not only is she a "lily of the valley," she is willing to run and bless the other lilies also. Budding vines and blooming pomegranates speak of the maturing stages of ministries. First the new growth, then the buds, afterward the fruit.

The Shulamite is no longer critical of the immaturity of other ministries; she is quick to recognize their strengths, their growth, and potential for fruitfulness. Every maturing saint will embrace the budding vines of ministries that are immature or limited in some way. How prone we are to exalt ourselves! Those who have been humbled by the Spirit will always see new growth, not just old wounds.

It is wrong to despise the ministries of others. Paul pronounced blessing on other ministries that criticized and condemned him (Phil. 1:15-18). The Holy Spirit will not allow us to be impatient with others, despising their immaturity. An unrelenting gratitude will fill the heart of the radiant Bride. We cannot be impatient with others when we remember our own history! God is raising up a people who will love and embrace the entire Body of Christ. Not only those we are comfortable with, but the entire Body of Christ in all her diversity.

Many are disgusted with the "budding vines" of ministries who are different, perhaps even abrasive to our unbroken flesh. But in every immature ministry (and every immature believer) there are virtues that are just beginning to bud. Filled with love for others, we can weep like Joseph over our brothers who wounded us in their ignorance (Gen. 50:15-21).

Mature Intercession

"My desire set me among the royal chariots. . . . " Before she realizes it, her intercession lifts her up in ecstatic joy and sets her among the glorious royal chariots. The chariots of God are swift and powerful, transporting the soul. Another translation of "royal chariots" is *"the chariot of Ammi-nadib."* Some commentators believe Ammi-nadib was the name of one of Solomon's celebrated chariot drivers. Ancient Jewish interpreters translated this, *"the chariots of my willing, princely people."* She is caught up into the delights of the spirit realm through her fervent intercession.

Suddenly, her enthusiasm for others has moved her soul swiftly like a chariot. Mature love has broken through. She is in a place of intensity and zeal for God to move among others. The spirit of intercession has fallen upon her!

"Come back, that we may gaze on you. . . . " The maiden has left to go to the Lord's garden and bless others. The sincere daughters cry out four times, "Come back," showing the intensity of their desire to be near her. Mature saints are the glorious ones, the truly attractive ones to others in the Body of Christ. For those with immature faith, it is sometimes easier to see Jesus through the mature ones. She has released the fragrance of Christ among them. They long to have her example in their midst. They see her love for the weak, immature, struggling believers and wish for her to stay and impart more of her mature love to them.

This is similar to Paul leaving the Ephesian elders in Acts 20:15-38. They too wept as Paul was taken from them to fulfill his destiny. How beautiful is this Bride!

The Dance of Angels

Now, the Beloved Bridegroom speaks to the sincere daughters . . . *the Shulamites-to-be.* Jesus questions those gazing at His Bride with this rhetorical question . . . **"Why would you gaze on the Shulamite as on the dance of Mahanaim?"** He is asking, "What do you see in her? Is it like watching the dance of angels?" The soon-to-be Shulamites will answer this question in Chapter 7.

Mahanaim was the place Jacob was left alone as he waits for his older brother Esau. They had quarreled years earlier when Jacob deceived his father and brother, stealing the birthright through trickery. At Mahanaim, Jacob was being pursued by Esau. Jacob encountered two companies of angels while at this place, so he named it Mahanaim ("two camps" or "two armies").

The angels of the Promised Land formed a welcoming committee to bless Jacob as he returned to his inheritance. Jacob was the Old Testament prodigal son who was coming back to his Father's House of Promise. The angels encircled Jacob and danced for joy over his return.

These two camps of powerful angels would provide Jacob's protection from his angry brother. Jesus refers to the dance of angels as He gazes upon His radiant Bride. Just as Jacob saw this dance as he returned to the Promised Land, so the Bride is dancing with angels as she begins to walk in the fullness of her inheritance. Truly she is beautiful in his eyes. . . . Like one dancing in victory with the angelic host!

This Jesus' Song is easy to dance to!

---

[1] This can also be translated "princesses."

[2] The "queenly" anointing is the least in number but has the greatest glory. Those virgins without number comprise the countless saints of God holding lesser degrees of glory. All the ones before God are accepted, loved, and treasured; but there are apparently varying measures of the glory of God that rest upon His servants.

"*How beautiful you are*
and how pleasing,
O love, with your delights!"

Song of Songs 7:6

☙ℭ

Delighted with Her Beauty

Chapter 7:1-10
ဢၣ

As Jesus comes forth in His church, He will turn our hearts to the poor of the earth. The nations must know Him. Passion for Jesus will eventually bring us to the place of serving others. Revival will transform the vision and destiny of the church. . . . Jesus is a Prophet whose Words will all come to pass. Are you ready for the greatest revival that the world has ever seen? Listen to the prophecies Jesus speaks over the end time church. . . .

Jesus has asked the daughters of Zion, those who have accompanied the Shulamite in her journey, "Why would you gaze on the Shulamite?" They will answer with a marvelous description of the maturing Bride. In fact, it is a prophecy. It is the Spirit of God speaking through them, revealing the glory of the King shining through His Bride.

The maiden gave a tenfold description of the glory of the Bridegroom (5:10-16), now the King gives a tenfold prophetic declaration over His Bride. What tenderness is in the heart of this King! Her beauty has captivated Him. He is releasing more and more of His life and beauty to her. She is reflecting the qualities of His endless life!

These ten prophecies will be fulfilled in the church before Jesus returns. They are descriptions of virtues and strengths that He will supernaturally deposit within her. Essentially, what follows is a practical definition of godliness and virtue that will arise like a shining light within the church.

This is the second time the King describes the Bride in detail. In 4:1-5, He gave eight affirmations beginning with her head . . . here He now gives ten affirmations beginning with her feet. These prophecies are meant to be a practical challenge to our growth in God.

In what follows, God is giving us a prophetic "road map" for spiritual growth coming to the end-time Bride. These prophetic virtues will be seen in her as the church gives herself to bridal passion in pursuit of the Son of God. Ask God to give you these attributes. Let them become fuel for your intercession. Cry out for your life, for your church to manifest these traits. . . .

1. The Good News Shoes —*"How beautiful . . . your sandaled feet"*
Beautiful feet in sandals speak of evangelism. Paul wrote to the Ephesians about the church whose feet were shod with readiness to preach the gospel of peace (Eph. 6:15). The maiden is now swift to take the gospel to others. A spirit of evangelism is flowing in the church. "How beautiful on the mountains are the feet of those who bring good news, who proclaim peace. . . . " (Isa. 52:7).

It is our inheritance to evangelize and claim spiritual territory with the soles of our feet (Josh. 1:3). Winning souls to Jesus Christ will be the joy and delight of the Bride as she begins to shine as a burning lamp for the nations. She had taken off her shoes in 5:3, now she is wearing the beautiful sandals of reaching the lost. O, the beautiful, dancing feet of the Shulamite!

Her feet are not bare as a beggar's. She has the "good news shoes" upon her feet—shoes that can walk upon the rocky hearts of men in evangelism. This is the church in militant victory, clothed with the wardrobe of warfare. Evangelism is a form of spiritual warfare as we tear down strongholds of unbelief and false religion in the hearts of mankind. The gospel is the power of God to bring deliverance and freedom to the lost (Rom.1:16).

"How beautiful"—The church will be powerful and successful in evangelism as the Bride flows as one with the Bridegroom. Her labors will be fruitful as the anointing of the Bridegroom is seen upon the mature Bride. She is in love with the King! This makes her beautiful to the nations! Someday they will all see the beauty of the Lord Jesus upon the feet of those that are swift to speak of Him!

"O Prince's daughter"—The Bride is the daughter of the Prince of Glory! She is the Princess Bride! With royal grace she moves out to win the nations and shine the light of Christ upon every dark corner of earth. By the new birth, she is linked in spirit and in virtue to the Prince. Everyone can see it now; The church is a Royal Priesthood. The blood of Jesus has touched us, making us kings who are priests, and priests who are royalty (I Pet. 2:9, II Cor. 6:18, Rev. 21:9). (See also Psalm 45.)

2. Her Graceful Walk—*"Your graceful legs are like jewels"*

The King sees the legs or thighs of the Bride and notices their dignity and grace. Her legs speak of her walk in power and wisdom. In 5:15, Jesus' leg (walk) was seen as a pillar. Here, the declaration over her is

"Your graceful legs are like jewels!" Muscular and shapely, her walk is in the power of the One who loves her and gave Himself for her.

Through the disciplines of the Spirit she has developed the leg of an athlete. Like the price of a costly jewel, she has paid the price of walking with Him in the high places. Jewels also remind us of the wisdom and revelation of the Spirit by which she does the work of the Lord (Prov. 8:11).

"The work of a craftsman's hands." Jesus is the skilled Craftsman! He has formed us, shaped us, made us, broken us, healed us, and filled us. The touch of His finger has touched our thigh as it did with Jacob. Even with "Jacob's limp," we are still God's "craftsmanship," or literally, "poetry" (Eph. 2:10). As the Master Poet, He has written the rhymes of heaven upon our human spirit. His Divine handiwork in the church will one day be seen by the universe.

The love of our King has strengthened us and prepared us for end-time ministry. His walk of wisdom and power will be broadcasted by the church! Our lives have been charted out ahead of time! Our God is not a haphazard Sovereign—He has purposefully shaped our walk to fulfill the destiny He has chosen for us! (See Eph. 2:8-10, 3:9-11.)

3. Her Inward Life — *"Your navel is a rounded goblet"*

Her navel speaks of her inner life. This inner life is the result of her attachment (umbilical cord) to the life and Spirit of the Lord. Her innermost being is flowing with rivers of living water (John 7:37-39). The inner life of the mature Bride is like a goblet of blended ("spiced") wine is. She is full of the wine of the Holy Spirit, serving joy and refreshment to others. Her life in the Spirit is rich, abundant, overflowing, blended, and never lacking! A fountain has opened up within her. This prophecy will be seen as the church is connected to Christ and flows forth with His fullness!

This ever-flowing **"blended wine"** speaks of the full-range of nourishment she is giving to the nations. Maturity in her inner life brings a blended (balanced) beverage to the thirsty hearts around her. Are you one who overflows with rivers of refreshment to others. So often we drain life from others instead of give life to the poor. . . . Lord, make us your goblet of blended wine for the joy of others!

4. <u>Giving Birth to a Harvest</u> — *"Your waist . . . a mound of wheat"*
A mound of wheat in Scripture is a vivid picture of the abundance of the coming harvest. This is a prophetic declaration that the harvest is birthed from the harvest! **"Waist"** can also be translated *womb*. From the womb of the mature Bride comes a harvest of wheat, not tares. Like a pregnant belly, the mound of wheat is beginning to show! She has been eating the hidden Manna of Revelation 2:17! She is bread for the nations as the harvest bursts forth from her inner life! Wheat also points us to the Bread of God, the Words of Eternal Life (John 6:33, 51, 68).

"Encircled by lilies." The harvest that comes forth from the Bride will be established in purity like a lily. This incredible harvest will be set about with holiness, bridal love, purity of heart, and passion for Jesus.

5. <u>Power to Nurture Others</u> — *"Your breasts are . . . two fawns"*
Her breasts speak of the ability to nurture and edify the young ones. As she gives birth, she will release a love and care for the young ones, nurturing babes by the milk of the Word. She is prepared now

for birthing the harvest and blessing those she wins to Christ. Fawns are tender and youthful, energetic and able to run and skip with the Lord of Glory. Twins speak of a double portion of grace to edify and establish new believers.

6. Her Determination — *"Your neck is like an ivory tower"*

In 4:4 He described her neck as the "tower of David," now it is **"like an ivory tower."** An ivory tower speaks of protection, a place of rare and costly uprightness. She will pay the price for being tall and beautiful in the sight of the nations. Like a lighthouse of ivory she will shine the light of Jesus to the nations. The neck is a picture of the will of the heart. Her neck like an ivory tower is a word picture of her resolute determination that has become her protection from evil. She has become a strong refuge against the enemy for others.

7. Her Clear Revelation — *"Your eyes are . . . pools"*

The eyes of her understanding have been enlightened in answer to the apostolic prayer of Ephesians Chapter One. Her faith and revelation have grown, spiritual insight characterizes her life. Beloved, the Church of Jesus Christ will soon walk in the light of Jesus Christ, in the knowledge of His ways! Her "dove's eyes" have now become pools!

"The pools of Heshbon" were known as some of the cleanest pools in the land. The city of Heshbon was the royal city of the Amorite King Sihon (Num. 21:25-26). The Bride's vision and revelation in the Spirit are pure; her insight can be trusted. The words she speaks to others are timely and refreshing.

No longer like muddy pools her discernment has been cleansed of the flesh. Her spiritual vision is a reservoir of revelation. She will make her judgments based on the love revelation He gives her, not from a heart of impurity. Heshbon can also mean "stronghold." She spoils the kingdom of darkness with her knowledge of the Lord.

"By the gate of Bath Rabbim" or *"the unique daughter among many."* As the multitude of nations looks into the eyes of the radiant Bride, they will see pure revelation, grace and deep calm. Many will drink from her pools.

8. Her Spiritual Discernment—*"Your nose is like ... "*

The nose speaks of the ability to "sniff out" the enemy and know where he is at work. She has grown in her discernment and is effective in spiritual warfare. The tower of Lebanon was a watchtower built to detect the enemy's activities. It was also significant in the protection of the King's property (II Chron. 8:5, 9:15-16). Next to the land of Syria, this tower was crucial for the protection of Israel.

The Bride is always alert as she is constantly **"looking toward Damascus."**[1] Her supernatural discernment in spiritual warfare will be the source of protection from the schemes of the enemy. Without a keen discernment, we are all vulnerable to the strategies of darkness. This knowledge is not logic, subject to human reasoning, but spiritual discernment based on the Word of God. It transcends what is heard or seen; it will discriminate between what is from man, God, and the Devil. Precise battle plans will be granted to the seeking, sensitive Bride. Jesus will have a Bride that is alert, giving protection to the nations.

9. Her Pure Thoughts—*"Your head crowns you. ... "*

The head speaks of our thoughts and wisdom. The Bride has purity of thought and excellency of wisdom;

what grace is upon her! She is quick to bring her thoughts into the obedience of Christ as she tears down strongholds. The helmet of salvation and deliverance is upon her head like a crown. Filled with hope, she does battle against every high thought that opposes the wisdom of God (II Cor. 10:1-5).

"Mount Carmel" was considered one of the most excellent and beautiful peaks in the land. Her fruitful wisdom and purity of thought can now be compared to the mountain of Carmel. Carmel can mean "crimson," the color of the blood of Christ. The Bride is a redhead! She is covered by the crimson blood of the Bridegroom. Mount Carmel was the place that God sent fire as an answer to Elijah's prayer. The thoughts of the Bride are victorious, like Mt. Carmel. The crown speaks of dominion and power over her foes. Jesus will have a Bride that has a pure and irresistible wisdom.

10. <u>Her Dedication to Jesus</u> — *"Your hair is . . . royal tapestry"*
    The royal heart of abandoned love fills her . . . the devotion of her life is unmistakable. The "royal (purple) tapestry" was exquisite in detail — and so is her heart of love for Him! She is highly desired and rare in His sight as she adorns His throne room like purple drapes. Even the angels are in awe of this one shining like the sun. She comes forth from her trials, unshakable in her consecration to heaven's Christ. **"The King is held captive by its tresses."**

Can you imagine the King of Glory being held captive as He gazes on the locks of her hair, or the depth of devotion coming from her heart? In the face of her resolve to do the will of God no matter what it costs her, Jesus is filled with delight and affection. He is overcome, held captive, imprisoned in her love! Your love captures a King! You are why He died on a

Cross. It is the joy of our Lord to be captivated in Holy Love for His Bride.

Like Jacob clinging to the Wrestling Man, her heart clings to Him until undying love prevails over His heart and holds Him captive! She is all He can think about. They are meant to be together forever, Bride and Bridegroom. No more foxes to spoil the vines, no hidden compromise, and no unwillingness to arise when He calls her. She's filled with Royal Love for the King. Jesus will have a Bride that is as devoted to Him as He is to the Father.

Pleasing to The Son of God

"How beautiful you are and how pleasing. . . . " The graceful, dancing, radiant Bride! Look at her as she arises to embrace the Bridegroom who is a King! Beautiful, pleasant, delightful, pleasing. . . . She is being conformed into the image of the One she loves so fervently. Love has transformed her heart. He is completely satisfied with the many charms of His own Nature coming forth within her (Isa. 62:4, Zeph. 3:16-17, Mal. 3:12). Jesus lifts His Song of Songs to a higher key and rejoices over her with singing! He uses the same words she spoke over Him to describe how He sees His Bride. . . . Can you take in the depth of His love?

The Lord so enjoys the fruits of bridal love and obedience from you and I! It is a pleasure to Him beyond our understanding. The way the King in our story loves the Shulamite is truly how the Lord feels about you. This is not a matter of unrelated doctrine. This is about you being loved by Jesus while you are still on earth. We think God is weary of us, tired of our unyielding ways, but He calls us beautiful even in the midst of our struggle to overcome sin. Just think of Jesus sitting next to you, tapping you on the shoulder, looking you in the eyes and saying these words, "How beautiful you are; I am not disappointed with you I am delighted in you."

"O love, with your delights!" This is Divine Romance! Jesus is enthralled, ravished, and passionate for His Bride. Jesus is expressing the depth of the unconditional love filling His heart.

Our love truly delights the holy heart of Jesus Christ. He enjoys our prayer life; He is thrilled each time He view us turning from evil. The radiance of our faith, the contentment we find in Him . . . all of this enraptures the Son of God.

When you think of love's delights, you and I usually think of how it pleases our heart. But what pleasure floods Jesus Christ as you break your heart open to Him and give Him the treasures of your worship! How can you say your life is not significant if you understand that the purpose of life is to give Him pleasure? You really are one of the *"glorious ones in whom is all His delight"* (Ps.16:3).[2] Jesus will have a bride that is pleasurable and utterly delightful to Him.

"Your stature is like that of the palm." Her stature speaks of her maturity. The palm tree is a symbol of victory in the Scriptures.[3] The children waved palm branches at the victorious entry of Jesus into Jerusalem. We are given gifts and graces of the Spirit to bring us into the stature of the fullness of Christ. She is bearing His image and growing into His fullness.

What victory surrounds her! Her life is upright, not twisted. She reaches for the heavens, knowing that is where her life is found (Col. 3:1-4). Her hidden life (roots) causes her to bear fruit and remain green and strong. All of her trials have only made her grow taller. She has the capacity to endure the dry seasons of life (Joel 1:12).

"Your breasts like clusters of fruit." The maiden is now a fully developed bride, the palm tree of the Lord. Her breasts are not only giving milk to nurture, but clusters of life giving fruit. The affections of her heart are full as she bears clusters of fruit for the blessing of others. These are the sweet fruits of spiritual maturity: discernment, gifting, anointing, grace to feed others. *Clusters* of sweet fruit now adorn her life.

"I will climb the palm tree. . . . " This is the declaration of the Bridegroom that He will be united in power with the Bride. In Acts 2, Jesus climbed the palm tree! This is a prophetic promise of end-time revival. The Son of God is ready to take over the church, filling its branches with His power.

Jesus will ascend the tree of His planting Rise up, O Lord! God has resolved to release revival power through the branches of this tree. Beloved, we are those branches! Jesus will once again lay hold of us in order to manifest His presence to the nations.

Signs and wonders are coming from the One who will take hold of us and make us His rod of might and wonder. Branch-life will greatly increase in coming days (Isa. 4:2). He will own the fruit as that which flows from Him. This shows the strong desire of the King to apprehend the "palm tree bride." This verse is an incredible prophecy of what is to come. . . .

Jesus now gives her a prophetic commission to a threefold demonstration of His power: **"Clusters . . . fragrance . . . best wine."** This will be the impact of taking hold of the branches and sending revival. . . .

1. **"May your breasts be like the clusters of the vine."** Jesus releases her to nurture the souls that will come in the great harvest of the nations. He prophesies of her ability to bless and strengthen many by the power

of the Spirit. The wine of the Holy Spirit will flow through her!

2. **"The fragrance of your breath like apples."** The breath speaks of her inner life. He prophesies that she will release the refreshing of the Holy Spirit. Just as God breathed into Adam (Gen. 2:7) and Jesus breathed on His disciples in the upper room (John 20:22), the end-time church will release (breathe) the power of the Spirit bringing revival to the nations. What is imparted will be a fragrance like apples, sweet and pleasing. The church will not have bad breath! She fed herself on the apples of His presence (2:3), now she has His breath to release to others. She has tasted and seen that the Lord is good. The revived church will breathe upon the dry bones of Ezekiel 37!

3. **"Your mouth like the best wine."** Throughout the Song of Songs, the mouth speaks of intimacy with Jesus. She prayed in 1:2 "Let Him kiss me with the kisses of His mouth." The Lord Jesus prophesies to the church that our intimacy with Him will be like the best wine. He has saved His best wine for last, and He freely shares it with His bride. The excellency of the Holy Spirit; the sweetest intimacy of the human spirit will pour like wine through the end-time church.

This is why Jesus turned water into wine at a wedding, to teach us of a greater wedding feast to come! We will grow to the place where we satisfy Him like nothing else. He will empower us in this place of intimacy. Jesus calls intimacy with you the best wine of all. . . . The most pleasurable thing outside of the Godhead is this love relationship between Christ and His Bride.

These prophetic declarations will empower us to remain intimate lovers of the Son of God. Her breasts, her breath, her mouth; the revived church will nurture others, release the power of the Spirit, and impart sacred intimacy. The kiss of this passage is far different than the kiss of 1:2; this is *a kiss of restoration*. It is the kiss of the Father to his prodigal son who returned to his house (Lk. 15:20). Here, the King is giving her the depths of His redeeming love. He smells her breath and gives her a kiss to empower her. We need more than one kiss! We must be those who rely on the love of God (I John 4:16).

Her Deep Feelings of Love

Jesus is interrupted by the maiden as she cannot hold it in any longer . . . she must tell Him how she feels at this time. **"May the wine go straight to my Lover. . . . "** He has told her that intimacy with her is the best wine of all . . . and now she must speak. She desires more than anything else to have a life that will never resist the Holy Spirit. The wine of the Spirit is to bring satisfaction not only to us, but to Him.

Did you know that the Holy Spirit fills you for Him? With this wine of bridal love in our hearts, we are able to love Jesus as He deserves to be loved. The Spirit's work within us is to satisfy Jesus. When we resist the Holy Spirit, we are robbing the Son of God of the joy of victory in our lives. Everything God does in a human heart is to glorify and satisfy Jesus! The "cup" of God's will goes down smoothly when we realize it is for "my Lover."

"Flowing gently over lips and teeth." The Holy Spirit flows gently in our hearts. Yes, He is like a River that is rushing, but the Spirit flows like wine, gently over lips and teeth. This phrase can also be translated, "moving gently the lips of sleepers." The wine of His love will revive those who are spiritually asleep, unaware that He is near. It arouses the spirit until our lips move with praise and longing for Him. The Spirit will use the mature Bridal Partners of Jesus to awaken desire in the hearts of sleeping saints. Spirit inspired speech will edify, challenge, exhort, and stir with passion the hearts of others.

"I belong to my lover, and His desire is for me." Behold the love of the Shulamite! Every other desire is lost in this love. She has become His Promised Land, His inheritance (Eph. 1:18). Her Lover owns her heart. He is all she cares about. Before now, fears and anxieties controlled her. All of life has now been given to Him alone.

It is a wonderful day when your identity becomes one that belongs to Him and not to yourself, your spouse, your family, nor your church. We belong to the One who loved us out of sin into salvation. This confession of our identity releases our inner man to love Him even more. . . .

Our heart breaks through the barrier of cold love when we speak these words, **"His desire is for me!"** As we go into the heart of Jesus, we gain insight into His affections toward us. The longings of His heart are really for us. Jesus lies awake at night thinking about His Bride. The thoughts He has toward you are more than could be numbered (Ps. 139:17-18). He has engraved you on the palms of His hands (Is. 49:16). How could He ever forget one that has been inscribed on His palm?

The desires and longings of the Son of God are toward you even when you have forgotten about Him. His desire is ever toward you. Understanding this awakens an even deeper abandonment to Him. This is why we love Him, because He first loved us (I John 4:19).

If we could really take this to heart, it would destroy depression. To know that His desire is toward us would change our lives significantly. When we are accused wrongly and misunderstood, we can say, "His desire is for me." When we are criticized and slandered by others, we can say, "His desire is for me." Our source of emotional security is wrapped up in His statement of love over us. Our spirit jumps up and down inside when we hear it. . . . "He really likes me!"

If God's desires are toward you, no one can defeat you. Even your weaknesses will not turn you back when you can say, "His desire is for me." John, the beloved apostle, described himself as the "one Jesus loved." This was not to say that John was loved more, or to the exclusion of the other disciples, only that he identified himself in the love of God. Love taught him to say this. Can you say today, *I am the one Jesus loves?"*

On the night Jesus was to be betrayed and beaten, He told His disciples of His desires for them. Knowing they would abandon Him and run . . . knowing they did not have enough strength to stand with Him in His hour of trial . . . His desire was still toward them. The affirmation of love comes to the weakest one, just like it comes to those who are faithful under pressure. Jesus' love for you is a torrent of passion that will not be turned aside because you fail Him. Nothing can separate you from His yearning love. It is impossible to be valued more than this.

Where is your focus today? Do your affections belong to your Lover, or have you spent them somewhere else? Do you see yourself alive on earth for His pleasure alone? Are you committed to whatever He desires? Let the fire of *His desires* tenderize your heart. . . . Hold your cold heart before the fire of His love until you can say, "I belong to my Lover and His desire is for me!"

[1.] Damascus is the capital city of Syria, Israel's greatest foe.

[2.] David knew that God delighted in him even while he was in fear and unbelief, stumbling in the city of Ziglag (Ps. 18:19).

[3.] The palm stands upright with deep roots, so is the life of the victorious over-comer. The palm raises its beautiful crown to the heavens. It is described as one of the ornaments of Solomon's Temple. See also Revelation 7:4.

"Let us go early to the vineyards

to see if the vines have budded,

if their blossoms have opened,

and if the pomegranates are in bloom;

there I will give you my love."

Song of Songs 7:12

&OCR

Leaning on Her Beloved

Chapter 7:11–8:12
ଊୠଔ

$\mathcal{H}$er Divine Journey into the heart of Jesus is nearing an end. Grace has brought her safe thus far and grace will lead her home. . . . What tenderness she has discovered, what tender response she has given to Him. Everything He has told her is now bearing fruit. The One who stretched Himself out on a Cross for her now stretches Himself out in fullness within her. She is learning to lean. . . . The two are becoming One. . . .

This time, she will leave her comfort zone when He bids her come. **"Come, my Lover, let us go. . . . "** Now she is ready to run with Him to the tops of the mountains and through every valley. The revelation He imparted in 7:5-9 has deeply changed her. A fresh commitment has been born to fulfill the Great Commission, touching the nations in His power. "Come" she cries out! His promise was (7:8), "I will come." Therefore, as the awakened Bride, she intercedes with the words, **"Come, my Lover!"** His promises are meant to be fuel for intercessory fire.

The book is now coming to a full circle. . . . In the beginning the King was drawing her, now she is drawing Him. She is interceding for the villages and needy places of the earth to know this King! She was invited to join

Him; now she invites Him to join her. "Let us" is used four times in 7:11-12. They are about to go forth in mature partnership (Mk. 16:20, I Cor. 15:10).

In the early days of her journey, she was behind her wall, sitting on the couch, or at the Banquet Table enjoying Him. He would come and ask her to follow Him. Each time, she refused. Convinced it would cost too much, her thoughts were . . . *"but I might fail."* Now, at the end of her journey, she is fearless. The dark trails no longer frighten her. She is willing to spend the night in faraway villages. As long as He is there, she has no fear of leaving the comfort zone. Her faith and obedience have grown. . . .

The nature of a pilgrim is coming forth from within the Shulamite. Now she is content to go with Him from village to village, seeking lost and wounded sheep. Now she is content to be a stranger to this world system, for she is truly free. Her confession is that of Ruth, "Wherever You go I will go, wherever You lodge, I will lodge. Your people are my people." The *countryside* speaks of the mission fields of the earth (Ps. 96:12-13, Prov. 31:16); the *villages* represent local churches. She intercedes and asks for His manifest presence as they co-labor together.

The Hebrew word for "villages" may also be translated as "henna bushes." She pleads with Him to go and touch the world as they sleep among the henna bushes. Remember, the word for "henna" is the Hebrew word *kaphar,* meaning "to make atonement." The mature Bride is willing to run to the ends of the earth to bring the message of love to those who have never heard.

The end-time Bride will run with Jesus to those places where redemption is ready to be released to the people groups of the earth. This is the ministry of reconciliation that the Bride presents to the unbelieving world

(II Cor. 5:17-21). The two have become One, and the entire world will feel the impact of that union.

The Shulamite is now thinking of others with compassion. **"Let us go early to the vineyards. . . . "** No longer selfish, she is longing to bless others she once disliked. Her desire is to see others succeed and blossom in the purpose of God. We must all realize that we are *all* important to Him. The heart of Jesus is thrilled over every local church—even those who have wounded you. Only the mature can run with Him in tenderness of heart to the villages of the Body of Christ.

"Let us . . . see if the vines have budded, if their blossoms have opened. . . . " At one time, He came to see if her vine was budding (6:11), now they will go together to visit the needy and immature, to see their newly budding virtues. The anointing of Jesus causes the vine to bud. It was in the Holy Place that Aaron's rod burst forth with budding life when left overnight before God. When we go with Jesus, His presence causes life to spring forth.

I once had a dream where Billy Graham came to me. We were together in a revival meeting where I was speaking. In the dream I had just preached to thousands . . . I was elated! But when I had finished ministering, Billy Graham placed his hand on my shoulder and looked deeply into my eyes, saying, "Don't be proud, Brian. *Jesus Christ makes anyone look good!*" Beloved, when we run with Jesus under His anointing, He makes anyone look good. All our fountains are found in Him.

Eagerness and zeal have energized the Bride. She is willing to go **"early"** and minister to others. Sacrifice is no longer avoided. She will pay the price to touch others in His Name. She will joyfully experience the urgency, the inconvenience, and the diligence of ministry. She is looking like Jesus as they co-labor in ministry.

Jesus rose early, before the breaking of day to seek the Father. She is willing to rise early as the Proverbs 31 Bride as she toils for her Master. His kingdom business is her first priority. She labors not merely for herself, but for others. . . . How deeply the Cross has dealt with her!

The budding vines speak of the churches/ministries that are immature, not fully grown in the ways of Divine grace. She has love to share, fruit to impart, and gifts to empower. Eager to present others *"perfect in Christ"* (Col. 1:28), her cry is to bless them — freely she has received and now freely she will give. Her heart is turned toward cultivating the garden of God in others. This is apostolic grace equipping her for ministry.

At first, she lamented that others had made her a keeper of the vineyard, wearying her with their work. Now she joyfully serves others in the vineyards out in the countryside. Because she loves Him she is feeding His lambs (John 21:15-17). During her immature years, serving others became a distraction from her enjoyment of Him. Ministry was a hindrance. But now, in full union with Him, she has become a vessel possessed by His life. . . . Ministry cannot distract her or separate her from His presence! She is His chariot of fire!

"There I will give you my love." *There*, in the place of giving her life for others. In the place of sacrificial service among the immature budding vines . . . where she risks persecution and injury. Away from her comfort zone, out in the countryside — *there* she gives Him her undistracted love! Even in the midst of labor, toil, pain, and disappointment in ministry . . .

Surrounded by spiritual warfare and conflicts, with fears within and pressures around me, yet I can say, *"There* I will give you my love!" The Father will prepare a Bride for Jesus who will not only love Him in a cozy church or in isolation from the tensions of life, but a Bride that loves Him in the hardest of times, in the hardest of places.

Some have translated this verse, "There I will give you my caresses." Can you give Him the sweetness of love in the midst of the battle? It is one thing to love Jesus in a cave, but it is only mature love that can keep our eyes on Him on the battlefield. True apostolic Christianity is coming. It will be seen in *sacred intimacy, sacrificial ministry,* and *faithfulness in suffering* (Phil. 3:10).

Nothing can diminish our love for Him when we are consumed with Holy Passion for Jesus. The hassles of ministry with the immature, the pressures and hardships of life—nothing will intimidate the victorious Bride. She is running with Him in Bridal partnership. Are you there yet? Are you running with the Son of God as He blesses the nations with His love?

Love Is In The Air

"The mandrakes send out their fragrance. . . . " The Bride is longing for love. Mandrakes were known as "love apples." They come from a small tree that yields little round aromatic apples. Purple in color and with a beautiful fragrance, they speak of royal love. They were believed to be an aid in bearing children, facilitating wedded love (Gen. 30:14-16).

Mandrakes bloom during wheat harvest. The Bride is working with the King to bring in the great harvest of souls. As she smells the mandrakes nearby, it reminds her again of the tender love He has shown her. She is not content to be just the Bride. She wants to become the mother of the King's child.

The Shulamite is seeking for the Son to be born in her. This is the longing of the church in these closing days of human history, to have Christ formed in us (Gal. 4:19).

This loving partnership will bear fruit. There will come a corporate expression of Christ on earth through the Bride that is in union with Jesus. This many-membered Body will be seen in the lives of a people that have died to self and are alive to God. Robed with the sun, the moon under her feet, and a crown with twelve stars on her head . . . the Bride will be with child (Rev. 12:1-2)!

"At our door is every delicacy." Their honeymoon house is nearby. As they enter, every delicacy imaginable is present. Love is in the air! Their glad experiences are shared as they labor together in the harvest! These are the pleasant fruits of a shared life, as the two partake together of grace and glory. Like delicacies to the soul are the fruits of yielding to His life within. In Him she now lives, in Him she moves, in Him she has her being.

"Both new and old that I have stored up for You, my Lover." She draws from deep experiences of the past and the ever-fresh revelation of today. O, the joys they share in partnership together! She does not come in from the harvest field empty-handed (I Thess. 2:19-20). These are the first fruits of the harvest, her wave offering! New experiences of mercy flow from the treasure house of Holy Love. Continuous harvest reaps continuous happiness (Lev. 26:10). Her treasures are stored up in heaven to be cast at His feet as her eternal love offering.

Her Love Grows Bold

"If I found You outside, I would kiss You. . . . " Looking Him in the eyes, she opens her heart to share a secret with Him. . . . **"If only You were to me like a brother. . . . "** She is concerned about her public display of affection. This was improper for her culture and her people. Public kissing was a violation of the standards of decency. The only exceptions to this were between blood relatives, such as between brother and sister. However, she longs to boldly show her loyalty and love to such a Marvelous King. If only He were a brother, she could be affectionate in public with no embarrassment, but He is her Lover!

The Bride longs for a full manifestation of their oneness in their relationship. She cannot hide her love for such a King. At the first, she would cry out for His kiss, now she would find and kiss Him! Others do not understand the passion of the church for One like Jesus. They mistake our abandonment to Him as foolishness. Even within the church, it is those who are most visible and outward in their affection to Jesus that bring up a religious spirit in the proud of heart. To see someone lavish their love on Jesus in a public worship service is disgusting to the self-righteous. The Bride prays for boldness to overcome the fear of what others think.

"I would . . . bring You to my mother's house. . . . " We usually think of the King leading us. How bold! We truly can bring Him to others through prevailing prayer and holy love. She longs to bring His presence into the Church, her mother's house (Gal. 4:26). His anointing is what they need and she knows it!

Jesus will actually let you lead Him! He gives you kingdom authority and He cooperates with your decisions. Only the mature will discover the fullness of this partnership of grace.

As an usher would lead one to the front row, the place of honor, so she desires to bring Jesus into the Church and usher Him into the highest place. Not content to kiss Him in public, she wants to bring Him back to the people who first taught her. She remembers those who have taught her and blessed her in the past, now she brings home the blessing of passionate love for Jesus!

"I would give you spiced wine to drink, the nectar of my pomegranates." She promises to serve Him the wine of her love. Wine mixed with spices is more expensive and more enjoyable; she will give Him her very best and costly adoration. She has become His very own cup of delight! We have the wonderful privilege of worshipping Jesus Christ. We have something sweet to offer Him each time our hearts open in praise. Our emotions are stirred, as they should be. Our hearts break open with perfumed praises. Sitting at His feet, we discover a union of spirit with the Son of God. This is how life is meant to be!

"His right arm embraces me." The full embrace of His love has come. He is able to love her completely, and embrace her for life in His loving arms. The displays of power with the right hand and the hidden demonstrations of care with the left hand hold her tight. The left hand is under her head, upholding her thoughts that she might rest in the assurance of His love. She no longer doubts His care, for He has come in answer to her prayer.

This embrace is what sustains the church. He holds us near to His heart when days of darkness surround the Bride. Have you hugged your Lord today? The arms that moved to shape a universe will move at the sound of your cry and hold you near.

Holding her like this, the King turns to the Daughters of Jerusalem as they stand nearby. . . . **"Daughters of Jerusalem, I charge you: Do not arouse or awaken love until it so desires."** Jesus will speak with authority to those who may misunderstand our love-embrace with the Bridegroom. We must leave this "charge" to Him. He is exhorting the maidens to refrain from disturbing her in this Divine moment of glory with the King. He has spoken these words three times in the Song, but this time He leaves out the phrase, "by the gazelles or does of the field." Her days of fear and timidity are over. She is caught up with Him, not with how it looks to others. Jesus will guard her in His grace until His purpose for her comes to pass, **"until it so desires!"**

Prophecy of the Victorious Bride

The voice of the Holy Spirit is heard as He prophesies of the victorious Church. **"Who is this coming up from the desert. . . .?"** She is seen coming up from the wilderness leaning on her Beloved. Who is this who has persevered through the wilderness testing, the lonely difficulties of life? There is nothing like the Bride in all of human history. She is a company of passionate people who have one goal for their existence . . . to be one with the Son of God! She has passed the tests of life. She has journeyed through the dark nights and hard trails. . . . She is His Overcoming Bride!

She is ascending, **"coming up from the desert."** She did not quit, but remained faithful. Love kept her heart faithful. Anybody will quit in the wilderness; only the one in love will stay true. Sometimes we have wanted to quit, but our love for Him kept us loyal. She will come up out of the wilderness no matter what, for she loves Him. The religious motivation of guilt, shame and fear are not sufficient, but love is. Her walk is ascension of the hidden stairway. Like the vision Jacob saw at Bethel, the Jesus-Stairway is before her. . . .

The Shulamite has walked up out of the desert into His end-time glory. She had been unable to leave the wilderness of spiritual wandering until she leaned on Him. Purified by fire, she is a Bride making herself ready for the eternal city. The Holy Spirit is prophesying her ultimate triumph by the power of God. Before Jesus was born, the Father promised the Son a Loyal, Leaning Bride. The Father arranged a marriage before the world was formed. You, beloved, are part of that loving company of virgins with one holy desire—to be one with Him.

"Leaning on her Lover" This is where we are meant to be; leaning on Him. With a loyal love her heart rests securely on His breast (John 13:23). He is her life source, her supply, her strength, her comfort, her Lover! God's desires for you will come to pass just as they have for the maiden. This prophetic declaration is to be sung as a Love-Song over you.

The day will come when all that is within you will be lost in Him forever! Song of Songs 8:5 is your destiny! The Lord's strategy throughout your life has been to produce in you an attitude of total dependency on Him (Jer. 9:23). Leaning, loving hearts will find no confidence in self, but will discover an endless Source of life in Him (II Cor. 3:5-6). As we lean, we absorb His life. It bleeds through. We begin to flow in His wisdom, not in our cleverness. We touch His power, not our feeble strivings. We are allowed to tap into unfailing love instead of our "love with strings attached." We must keep leaning harder and harder onto Him until it is asked with amazement, "Who is this . . . leaning on his/her Lover?" Notice the different ways we lean upon our Lover:

- **To be saved from sin.** We must lean on the Cross of our Beloved and find His blood as the only antidote for sin's guilt.

- **To live above the power of sin.** We lean on His life within us to conquer sin's power in our lives. Determination, discipline, prayer and godly friends all contribute, but only His indestructible life released in us can deliver us from sin. We leaning on Him for our victory. We are weak and insufficient. He is mighty and able to rescue!

- **To walk in emotional wholeness**. We lean on Him to be free from the wounds of our past and the difficulties of our environment today. He was bruised, rejected and despised, yet lived the most whole and balanced life. This will be released in our emotional make-up as we lean on our Lover. All the self-protecting "mechanisms" are abandoned when we lean on Him.

- **To receive guidance and direction for our lives**. Leaning on the Lord Jesus for wisdom will be the only sure way of discerning the will of God. He has the power to turn our hearts toward Him, causing us to *want* the will of God. He has the power to intervene in our circumstances, making them line up correctly with His purposes.

- **To be provided for and loved**. Jesus alone must be our source of supply. He is in our midst as One who serves. As we lean on Him we will have no lack. All good things come from Him who loved us and gave Himself for us (Isa. 41:17-20).

Our lives have been spent leaning on our own understanding, on our own clever ability to find a way out of every mess we get into. Often, the last thing we do is lean on Him. We have been taught to stand on our own, to become our own savior. We wander from Him, rather than lean on Him. But all of this is about to change. . . . The prophecy of the Holy Spirit has been sung over you. . . . You *will* come up out of your desert leaning on your Lover!

When you see Him as your Lover you will want to lean on Him! The Lord has used the desert to break you; it has served its purpose. Like Jacob leaning on his staff, you must lean on the Lord as you walk forward. Unable to plan your way, He is becoming the Light unto your path. The stubborn heart of stone has been replaced with a heart of flesh that responds to His gaze (Ezek. 36:26-27, Ps. 32:8, Prov. 1:23).

Reminded of Her Past

As a poor sinner, the Shulamite was sought by the Lord, discovered beneath the apple tree and loved just as she was. **"Under the apple tree I roused you. . . . "** The apple tree is a picture of Christ in the fullness of His love. Under the shadow of His eternal love, her Beloved awakened her to see the Cross.

If Jesus had not stirred *your* heart and roused *you* to seek Him, *you* would be lost. We owe it all to Him. It was the sovereign work of the Spirit of God that initiated our salvation and all spiritual progress in our lives. He comes to knock on the doors of our hearts to rouse us in holy passion for Jesus. God is the Author of our natural and spiritual birth.

The Lord is pleased to use us to rouse the hearts of others and confront them with their need for salvation. All of us heard the gospel from someone else. We become part of God's way of awakening sinners to Christ. God is our Father and the Church is like our mother. This is seen in the words "there she who was in labor gave you birth." The church labors through intercession and the preaching of the gospel, giving birth to converts (Rev.12:2). These converts then become the Daughters of Jerusalem until they are captured by Holy affections and begin their own Shulamite journey. . . .

The Fiery Seal Of Jealous Love

This is the wonderful invitation of Jesus to the mature Bride: **"Set ME as the seal over your heart."** Her journey began with a longing for kisses and ends with the fiery seal of Divine Love encasing her heart. He was the One who awakened her, and He will be the One to preserve her blameless in His love. This seal is for protection, preservation and passion. It is a seal of approval, of favor. It is a seal of ownership, for she belongs to the King! It is a Royal Seal that cannot be broken (breaking a royal seal meant certain death in the days of Solomon). This is not a seal made of wax, but a supernatural seal made of love. It is the power of supernatural love released in her heart by the Holy Spirit. Jesus invites her to place Him as that seal of love throughout her days.

As the Lord Jesus becomes the fiery seal over our hearts, we are progressively brought into the ownership of Jesus Christ. He possesses our souls, our feelings, our spirit, and our lives. This is the unfolding of the image of Jesus in the human spirit as He transforms our inner being. Divine love is the seal, not our past victories or discipline over the flesh. It is not our devotion to Him that seals us, nor is it our past failures; it is Him alone. This is the same terminology King David used in Psalm 16:8, "I have set the Lord always before me (as a seal over my heart). Because He is at my right hand, I will not be shaken."[1]

The Hebrew word for **"seal"** can also be translated, "a prison cell." The Lord Jesus wants to imprison us in His love. What a blessed prison is the seal of His love! Perhaps this is what Paul the apostle recognized in calling himself, *"the prisoner of the Lord"* (Eph. 4:1). In the prison cell of His love we discover that only His will and pleasure is our delight. Satisfaction comes when we abandon our small goals for becoming one with Him. How do we place Jesus as a fiery seal over our hearts? By communing with Him. As we place our hearts before Him, we take Him inside of us through Divine fellowship. He covers our hearts with a wedding canopy of love, thus sealing us from our foes and locking us into Him. He carries us moment by moment over His heart; now we must set Him as a Love-Seal over ours.

As you open your spirit to behold His love (I John 3:1), He releases Divine activity of the Holy Spirit within. We become one in a living, loving partnership with the Son of God. His love seals us tight! We give a permanent place for Him to dwell in . . . a palace of love!

Jesus is Our Secret Strength

"Like a seal on your arm." The heart is the place of love and the arm is where strength lies. Jesus wants to be a fiery seal over our affections and our strength. What we need the most, Jesus will supply—passion and power! Jesus Himself will seal our arms with Divine anointing and strength. We are enabled by His borrowed life to minister to others. The anointing is our secret strength. With sealed arms we can impart blessings and holy passion to others. As we minister with Jesus as the Seal on our arms, we are preserved from "burn out" in ministry. A spiritual buoyancy characterizes our ministries when our arms are sealed in omnipotent love. Supernatural grace just flows from the Seal upon our arms!

Our service is sanctified when Jesus is our secret Source of strength. We mount up with eagle's wings and run without weariness. The busy activities of the flesh only leave us exhausted, as we make futile efforts to do it all. In His strength, with our arms sealed in fiery love, every act of service flows from a more pure fountain. This twofold Bridal seal on our arms and on our hearts will be the joy of life. We can endure anything when our emotions and our strength flow out from His love.

The Seal of Eternal Love

How strong is death? There is no one who escapes its grasp. It is the king of terrors. All the tears and sorrow, the sighs of loved ones—nothing can free one who is held in its grip. Human power is hopeless in the face of death. . . . Who can escape its strong hold over this fallen world?

You cannot bribe death with money or persuade it to go away. Death watches over its victims and holds them in an unshakable vise. Nobody escapes. Death is a prevailing, comprehensive power. Once it holds you, it will not let you go. . . . *This is what God's love is like!* **"For love is as strong as death. . . . "** God's love holds you fast and will never let you go. You may run from His love, but it will seek you out. Relentless, omnipotent love will eventually win!

"Its jealousy unyielding as the grave." There is a power to the love of Jesus that claims everything. He is not content with a partial ownership of our hearts. His is a jealous love. Jesus walked in that love toward the Father. Zeal for His Father's House consumed Him (John 2:17)! The jealousy of His love is pure, a manifestation of intense longing to have us as His promised land (James 4:5, Eph. 1:18). It is His fiery envy to make us pure . . . for the Son of God.

What could be more cruel than the grave? It is unmoved by the tears of others when we lower our loved ones into the dark tomb of death. . . . The grave knows no pity, no sympathy. Just as the grave will not let go of its victims, so Jesus' love will not surrender you or let you go. You were meant for Him. Your journey is into His fiery, jealous heart of love. Never will He let you go! How intense is His love for weak, still struggling believers! Jesus is about to release a love to His Bride that is so comprehensive, so jealous, that it can only be compared to death and the grave. It will capture us in our failures and heal us completely. Never resting until we are perfected in grace, this love will operate through every pain and pleasure of life until we are like the Lord Jesus. The Father loved His Son so much, He decided to populate heaven with people just like Him! You might as well surrender now—His love will win in the end!

When Jesus gave Himself for us on the Cross, He was thinking of you. He was looking to the time when you would take Him as a seal upon your heart. For Him, the grave was not cruel; it was the means to find you. The last words of our Lord Jesus as He offered Himself to God were, "It is finished." Completed. Done. . . .

In the Aramaic language, the word Jesus actually spoke was *"kalah."* This has two meanings. One is, "finished or accomplished," and the other is *"bride."* The very last word of your King as He died for you was a sigh for His Bride . . . He died for His Bride!

Love's Fiery Flames

"It burns like blazing fire, like a mighty flame. . . . " The flashes of love that come from the heart of Jesus are like solar flares. The blazing fire of the Son of God will consume us in the end. We will be captured and ruined by His love. In the prison cell of love, fire surrounds us; its bolts are bolts of fire—furious flames! The very lightning of God will envelop our souls as He becomes the Bridal Seal. What kind of love is this? What kind of burning fire is His love? It burns like the flame of Jehovah, the burning fires of Almighty God! To touch love is to touch God, for our God is a consuming fire.

This mighty flame is nothing less than the very flame of Jehovah. Some Hebrew scholars have translated this phrase, "the very flame of Jah!" It is a supernatural burning of God in the soul (Luke 24:32, Isa. 4:4). One of the first revelations of God given in the Scripture is Deut. 4:24, "Our God is a consuming fire." He defines Himself as One with a hot, passionate love for His people that will consume and destroy every distraction from holiness.

God has fiery emotions. He is a passionate God who will baptize His Bride in the consuming ocean of His eternal love. When we think of God's fire, we think of judgment. But God's fire is first a fire of passion for His people. Jesus looks with eyes of fire upon His Bride (Rev. 19:12). This is not a fire of judgment, but a passionate, fiery gaze meant to consume us.

Undistracted devotion to Jesus will brand the heart with burning passions. Nothing can be compared to this love. Intense, unyielding, like a million nuclear reactors of blazing fire. . . . This is the seal He invites you to place over your heart! It is a seal that will brand you for life, forever changed by that love. It will consume your shackles and chains of emotional bondage and pain. It will unravel your clever ways and break the self-confidence that has been a part of your life.

When a love like this gets hold of you it is like the eruption of a holy volcano within you! The lava of His love will scorch your flesh life, burning up the dross of earthly ambition and pride. It is an unquenchable fire that will not rest until you are fully His.

Regardless of your sin or failure, this relentless love that consumes like a forest fire will defeat it! It is a tenderizing fire that will leave us responsive to Him, craving more. You are about to become His burning bush of fire (Ex.3:2)!

"Many waters cannot quench love. . . . " These waters are floods of obstacles and pressures. Nothing can put out the eternal flame of Divine love burning within the Bride. Water puts out fire, but *many* waters cannot quench this love! Even rivers of persecution cannot do it. Rivers of misunderstanding, heartache, disappointment, or pain cannot quench His love. Rivers of accusation, condemnation and rejection cannot put out the sacred flame. Joseph felt temptation, Peter denied our Lord Jesus, Saul of Tarsus persecuted the saints, but nothing could extinguish love's jealous flames.

This supernatural fire fell from heaven, consuming the living sacrifices of the Bridal company. It will not go out. Sickness, failure, divorce, shame and guilt—none of these can quench the love of God. He will never put out the fire that burns in our hearts. You can be fired from your job, kicked out of church, rejected by those you love; the strongest rivers of difficulty cannot put out this blazing fire (Rev. 12:16-17)!

His love is the seal, and the source of this love is God Himself. Our ability to claim this love has nothing to do with our temperament or personality, how we have treated Him or what we have done to mess up our lives. His love is the seal over our hearts, not our performance, not our devotion! His fire is greater than the illegal fires of sexual sin, pornography, or drug addiction. His fire will not be put out by your failure to walk perfectly before Him. His love is the seal, not your secret failures and shameful history. This love will prevail, it will conquer you in the end; you will be consumed in its flames! Love conquers all (I Cor. 13:8-13) and never fails. When you fail, love doesn't.

A Love Without Price Tags

Your life, your home, your wealth, your ministry—they are nothing compared to this priceless love. We would gladly give it all away to know a love like this! **"If one were to give all the wealth of his house for love ... "** This speaks of a man who would sacrificially give up everything he has to help the one he truly loves. This is a wholehearted love for Jesus. He is everything to one who loves Him. Everything else is to be **"utterly scorned."** This is the first commandment being fulfilled in a human life: to love Him with all of our heart, all of our mind and all of our strength. This is where the kisses of 1:2 will take us!

When you are in love you don't worry about the cost. A man will spend hundreds, even thousands of dollars on an engagement ring without a second thought. He has a love without price tags! A person in love does not worry about sacrifice. There is no limit to what a person in love will give. To call it a sacrifice is an insult.

Imagine having a child that could only be spared from death if you would sell your home, car, and your life savings — everything to pay for the treatment that could save her life. . . . Would you do it? Yes, if you love her you would. You would utterly scorn the "things" in order to have the one thing that matters most. You would not even consider it a sacrifice. It is all nothing compared to the life of your loved one. Love will prompt you to lay it all aside without regard to cost. . . . This is the love that will abide in the Bride as she is presented to Jesus on His wedding day!

Love moved Paul to write in Philippians 3:8, "I consider everything a loss compared to the surpassing greatness of knowing Christ Jesus my Lord." When love sacrifices, there is no loss. Put everything in life on one side of a scale, then put knowing Jesus on the other side; which would be the side to win your heart? When we taste the indescribable delight of knowing the Son of God, when we see His beauty and drink the wine of His love, we can live for nothing else.

If all the wealth of the world were to be given to you if you would deny Him, you would love Him still. If all the honor of the world were to be laid at your feet if you would deny Him, you would love Him still. Jesus is the reward of love. He is enough for every captured heart.

Ask the Lord to come upon your heart as a fiery seal. Ask Him to energize all your labors for Him as the secret source of strength. Ask Him to give you that sacred flame, burning with all its intensity until it consumes you. Ask Him to release a grace to love Him with all your heart, mind and strength, until the shadows flee and the night gives way to His brilliant Day!

The Bride Intercedes for the Immature

"What shall we do for our sister?" The Shulamite turns to look upon the other maidens and begins to intercede for others in the Body. With the seal of Bridal Love on her heart she grows in her concern for those who have yet to make the journey. There are still babes in Christ that do not know the depth of His love; they have yet to hear the "cooing of doves." What shall *we* do, she asks, "for **our** sister"? She has no private matters, no private relationships, no private interests. Everything is shared with the Bridegroom. She wants to know His thoughts about everything.

The Bride understands now that she has a responsibility to bless the young, immature ones in Christ. She is willing to partner with Jesus in laboring among the young sisters (Matt. 12:50). They have not yet cried out for the kisses and for the drawing; she will be the one to pray and show them the way. She must help them grow in the courage and confidence that He loves them in the midst of their weaknesses.

"Her breasts are not yet grown." This sister represents all that truly love the Lord Jesus but are underdeveloped and immature. She is not yet equipped to nurture and strengthen others, as a spiritual mother would nurse children in the body. Many in the church today are unable to be a source of encouragement and care for others, as they need constant care for themselves! Overwhelmed with their own problems, they have yet to develop and mature so they are able to richly bless others in the Body. Lacking character, patience, wisdom and discernment they are as yet unprepared for servant ministry in the church.

What should *we* do? We must pray as the Shulamite did and give ourselves to the "young" sisters and brothers. Our life vision must include preparing others to be part of the marvelous company called the Virgin Bride of Christ (II Cor. 11:2).

The wedding day for this young sister is coming and she is still unprepared for **"the day she is spoken for."** The Lord is about to come to this young sister and take her hand in marriage. Her courtship is about to begin. Our intercession prepares the way for ministry to touch and equip her with a passion to pursue Jesus wholeheartedly. In the day of God's visitation, He will require a measure of maturity from the "young" ones (Eph. 4:13). This is now the engagement time, but the wedding is at hand. We must labor to present a mature Body to Jesus on that day (Col. 1:28-29).

The Bridegroom replies . . . **"If she is a wall, we will build towers of silver on her. If she is a door, we will enclose her with panels of cedar."** Together, the Bride and Bridegroom will labor in intercession with a commitment to see the maturity of the "young sister." The King and His Queen are one! They work as partners, co-laborers for others.

The phrase, **"If she is a wall"** means, if she is one who is mature enough to defend herself from spiritual enemies, we will build towers upon her devotion. Cities with walls were well defended. Cities without walls were vulnerable to the attack of their foes.[2]

The Shulamite is saying that if we discern that she has grown enough to keep strong under attack, then we will build towers (watchtowers) or battlements of silver on top of her walls. This is a picture of taking her forward in her spiritual battles, helping her in the fight of faith and keeping her well protected. These silver towers will give her a redemptive viewpoint. She will be able to see where the enemy is coming at her and use the weapons of redemption (silver) to defend herself (Ps. 127:1).

This impartation of supernatural grace is meant to guard her from harm. With apostolic maturity, the Shulamite is ready to build towers in the lives of others. These towers will strengthen her in the Lord. With truth from the Word and the weapons of spiritual victory, she will endure the tests in her immature seasons. If she commits to being a wall that lives for the care of others, she will grow even more . . . but what if she is not a wall? What if she is a door?

"If she is a door, we will enclose her with panels of cedar." A door is a point of entry. Often in the Scriptures we read of a door opened for evangelism (Col. 4:3). Jesus opens doors that no man can shut (the grace to reach others with the gospel, Rev. 3:8). If she is found to be a vessel that opens the way of salvation for others, then we will enclose her with cedar panels.

To enclose her with cedar panels speaks of being clothed with Jesus Christ, clothed with power from on high. It speaks of the anointing that comes from the Lord through intercession to touch the nations with the gospel. If she consents to being a door of evangelism, we will pray down the power and anointing upon her to go!

Cedar panels are expensive, strong, and fragrantly scented. Cedars often speak of humanity. Jesus is the fragrant Cedar of Lebanon (3:9). Boards of cedar enclosing her life speak of the fragrance of the life of Jesus surrounding her labors. The cedars in the Temple were overlaid with gold (I Kings 6:20-22). Enclosed in Him, clothed with Jesus Christ, she will go to touch many for the gospel. This is being clothed with Jesus Christ.

Some ministries in the Body function as walls to protect and bless others. They are discerning the times accurately and are able to give much to others. Pastors and prophets are often like walls that give definition and care to local churches. Some ministries are like doors to new things. They are teachers and evangelists who open doors to evangelism and new truths. Some protect, some open doors; we need them both. But all must be passionate flames of fire for Jesus!

Again, notice what the King declares: **"We will build towers. . . . We will enclose her. . . . "** He will not carry out His purposes of grace without using the Bride. She will be His partner, His help-meet, His hands. They are one in love and one in labor. The sweetness of their union is complete.

What a picture we have here. The King is jubilant, the Bride is radiant, the Son is magnificent, the Daughters are joyous, and the young sister is resplendent with shining silver and fragrant with cedar. The work of redeeming grace is manifesting in the church. This holy family will shine forth, casting out darkness from the created order. The kingdom is coming. The Bride has a place at His side that no other may have. . . . She is His queen, His co-ruler over all things. She has made herself ready to sit with Him on the throne. She will bring forth the SPIRITUAL SEED that will crush the head of the serpent, as the Lamb's Wife dwells with Him forever!

---

[1] See also Ex.28:11 & Hag.2:23.

[2] God spoke to His prophet Jeremiah with these words, *"I will make you a wall to this people, a fortified wall of bronze; they will fight against you but will not overcome you, for I am with you to rescue and save you, declares the Lord."* Jeremiah 1:18-19

"You who dwell in the gardens
With friends in attendance,
Let me hear your voice!
Come away, my lover, And be like a
Gazelle or like a young stag
On the spice-laden mountains."

Song of Songs 8:13-14

৪৩

Conclusion:

The Happiest of Endings!

Chapter 8:13-14
ℰ℧ℭℨ

*W*hat a journey this has been! It is the mystical, mysterious journey of our soul into the heart of Jesus Christ. This is the great Song of Songs that will endure throughout eternity as the Song of the Lamb (Rev. 15:3-4)! Are you ready for another chorus of love?

The Shulamite's final declaration in the Song is a revelation of what she has become in His eyes. . . . **"I have become in His eyes like one bringing contentment."** Is this how you see yourself? Your Lover-King has made you into one that satisfies. . . . The seal of fiery love has transformed you from a "nobody" into a beautiful partner, a queen, worthy to share the throne of a King. It is time for the Bride of Christ to see herself as Jesus sees her . . . the delightful and desirable Bride who refreshes the heart of her Beloved.

"I am a wall and my breasts are like towers." She acknowledges that she is one of the mature ministries that exist to protect and bless others. She credits all her growth to the work of grace released by the seal of love on her heart. Like John the Baptist who could use his own ministry and maturity as a measurement of Jesus' works ("He is mightier than I"), and like Moses who could describe himself as the meekest man (Num. 12:3), so the Shulamite is able to describe her progress in real terms, yet without boasting (I Cor. 11:1).

As a wall, the stones and arrows would hit *her*, before they could harm others. She stands mature and faithful in the day of battle. How the church needs mature ones like her! She commits herself to enclose and protect the local churches (cities). She leads by example and stands firm on behalf of others.

Her breasts like towers speak of her great ability to nurture and give sustenance to many. Towers are seen from great distances, she has a trans-local sphere of ministry (Isa. 54:11-17). Now she has become one who has grown to a place of maturity, bringing great contentment to Jesus. His heart has longed for His flock to be cared for and protected. The Shulamite has become a shepherd after His own heart.

As she gives herself for others, the heart of Jesus is content and satisfied with her life. Her destiny is being fulfilled; she has found peace in His eyes. Like Mary, the mother of Jesus, she has found great favor with God.

A Parable of Accountability

"He let out His vineyard to tenants. . . . " This short parable (v.11-12) speaks of the accountability of the Lord's people. He will entrust us with stewardship in His vineyard and reward us accordingly. Every lover of God will one day stand before the judgment seat of Christ to receive reward or suffer loss (I Cor. 3:11-15, II Cor. 5:10, Rom.14:12-14). The figure of a vineyard is seen frequently in Scripture as the work of feeding, leading, and maturing God's people (Isa. 5, Matt. 25, John 15). The Lord of the vineyard will one day return and demand an accounting for what has been lent to us.

In this context, Solomon would refer to One greater than Solomon, our Lord Jesus. The vineyard of Baal Hamon speaks of the church of Jesus Christ that reaches throughout all the earth. The name **"Baal Hamon"** means, "lord of a multitude." Jesus is Master of many servants. Before the Lord returns, we expect a great harvest from among the nations, a multitude of souls redeemed by love (Rev. 14:14-16).

Solomon leased his vineyard to tenants, or keepers (Matt. 21:33). Jesus has given *us* the responsibility to keep His flock, tend His vines, and bring forth fruits of righteousness (I Cor. 3:9, Mark 16:20). Jesus is the rightful owner of the kingdom of God and may give the responsibilities of the kingdom to whosoever He wishes to tend. The caretakers of the Lord's vineyard will have the privilege and reward of bringing to Him the abundance of fruit from the maturing lives of those they shepherd. Precious fruit will come forth and be gathered to the Lord from the multitudes. As God gives the increase, the faithful labors of many will bear fruit.

"A thousand shekels of silver" represents the fullness of maturity that will spring forth from their labors. Isaiah 7:23 supplies an excellent commentary on this truth, "In that day, in every place where there were a thousand vines worth a thousand silver shekels, there will be only briers and thorns." The number one thousand speaks of the full measure of what God requires from His investment. Our Lord has given us all we need to bring forth fruit. He has given us talents, spiritual gifts and graces, and has anointed us to minister in His vineyard. We must till the soil, cultivate it, and tend it until it reaches maturity.

Jesus receives His thousand shekels of silver every time a life comes into the maturity seen in the maiden in the Song of Songs. The Shulamite can now say to the

King, "See, here are your one thousand shekels of silver (redemption), the mature ones that are fruit bearing vines in Your kingdom. Your Divine life now flows in them, as it does in me. We are branches united in love to You, the Vine of heaven." Listen to her words. . . .

"But my own vineyard is mine to give; the thousand shekels are for you, O Solomon" Her own life is fully given to Him as His life of fruitfulness and virtue shines in her. Her vine is worth a thousand shekels of silver, and now she gives Jesus all He expects from her. His work is complete; she is bearing His image. In 1:6 she was made a keeper of vineyards though she neglected her own. . . . Now her own vineyard is full and mature, bearing magnificent fruit. God wanted this fruit in Eden, now He tastes it in her.

"And two hundred are for those who tend its fruit" This double portion comes to the faithful elders who are worthy of their reward (I Tim. 5:17). Many are those who helped her in her journey . . . those who had gone on before her. They are to receive this portion of two hundred (fruit not shekels!). The Lord will not forget those who have labored in His Name (Heb. 6:10).

How wonderful is this journey. . . . How mighty is His love to carry her through! From a life of darkness under the sun to a life of fullness and glorious fruitfulness...this is the power of His grace. It has worked in her to do His good pleasure (Phil. 2:13). **Have you seen yourself in this journey?** Can you see what the King longs to do in you? Wherever you are on this journey, there is a burning fire blazing before you. . . . A love that will not let you go. Now is the time to end our journey together with the closing exchange of love between the maiden and the King. . . . It is a sacred ending, the happiest ending ever told. Content forever, the King and His Bride will become the Eternal City of Love and dwell together as One. . . .

Before we go, let us listen one last time to the King as He sings His love ballad over His Bride . . . and her response will be our parting prayer, **"Come."**

The King has a final desire filling His heart, **"Let Me hear your voice. . . . "** He longs to hear her voice, her intercession for His coming. How sweet is *your* voice to the Lord! It thrills His heart to hear you pray and speak with Him. Your voice has become a source of pleasure to the King.

If the Shulamite's voice was sweet to Him in her immaturity (2:14), how much more sweet is it to Him now that her devotion is complete as His Bridal Partner! Lifting our voices to Him in worship, adoration, and prayer ministers to His heart. To pray is to satisfy His longings. Does this give you a desire to pray? May our voices be ever sweet to Him! May our teaching and feeding of others be a sweet sound in His ears.

The King commissions the Bride to intercede and remain faithful to her Bridegroom until He returns to take her to an eternal honeymoon. She is called one **"who dwells in the gardens."** She is diligently laboring for Him in the gardens, for He may be found in many places. In the various aspects of equipping and tending the vineyard, she has remained loyal to Him. To make the garden her dwelling means that she has purposed to have a continued involvement in the Body. The King's title of her is one of great respect and honor. . . . She is occupied with His concerns! Truly, He is her garden. . . .

"With friends in attendance" Many are those who have received from her ministry, they are "friends" who will one day become a "Shulamite." They too, are listening to the voice of the Bride that they may learn of holy passion.

His final encouragement to her is this: "My precious darling, in all your labors and ministry to others, let Me hear your voice. Do not neglect the place of intercession and intimate prayer. This is my longing—to hear your voice!" Never let busyness, offense, tensions and pressures drown out your daily devotion to minister to the heart of Jesus. Let nothing stop your sweet voice from coming before Him.

Every time you whisper, "I love You, Lord" you are bringing the most precious sound to His ears. Let your cry for revival, your night and day intercession, be as a continual love song to the Son of God. Jesus, your Friend, asks for your fellowship in prayer. He longs for you to be a prayer-partner with Him in these last days.

The Song ends with the affirmation of Jesus over His Bride. Now we must hear her parting sighs as she longs to be with Him. . . . **"Come away, my Lover. . . . "**

She loves this King. She not only enthralls Him, she understands Him now! Her spirit erupts with a cry from her inner being . . . **"Come."** Urgency and longing are in her voice . . . like the groaning of creation longing for the manifestations of the sons and daughters of God. Until the shadows flee and the day breaks, her ceaseless cry will be, **"Come away."**

To be with Him is her victory, her dream come true! Fervent love has made her one with her Beloved Bridegroom-King. As Conqueror over every difficulty, Jesus, the young Stag, dances in exuberance over His Bride. Can you see this Lord of the Dance?

The Song of Songs ends as it begins. This time, she is leaping and running with Him. Her prayer has been answered. He drew her, now she runs after Him! She is echoing the very words He once spoke to draw her to the mountains. Now her desire is that He would steal away and run with her, dancing together upon the mountain-tops!

She has said, *"I do"* to the King. What Divine Partners they make . . . wooed and pursued. Spinning, twirling, skipping together. It is a marriage made in heaven.

They are Bride and Bridegroom forever, like gazelles leaping in resurrection power. Their love is as innocent as a spring morning, pure as a mountain spring. What joy they find together on the mountains of spice! Arm in arm they join together in the Ancient Dance before the Ancient of Days. . . .

Come away and skip again, O Mighty King. Dance in the gladness of your heart! Leap over the mountains as you did when you swept my heart away!

Just Married!

The "spice laden mountains" are peaks of pleasure
That we will experience together. . . .
Unspeakable happiness awaits us . . . forever.
FOREVER!

So they dance together in unbroken communion . . .
In the high places of the sky!
We too will one day skip with Him
Never to be separated. . . .

I love You my King!
You are my Lover-Friend!
I will never let you go! Never!
The Spirit and the *Bride* say . . .

Come!

Other Books by Brian Simmons:

GENESIS: The Spiritual Seed & the Ways of God

PRAYER PARTNERS WITH JESUS: Secrets of Intercession

DAVIDIC WORSHIP: David, His Tabernacle & His Psalms

Stairway Ministries
P.O. Box 26512
West Haven, CT. 06516
203-934-0880

Web Address: www.StairwayMinistries.org
Email: Stairwayministry@hotmail.com